Auld Enemies
The Scots and the English

Also by David Ross

Scotland: History of a Nation
The Killing Time: Scotland 1638–1707
Awa' and Bile Yer Heid: Scottish Insults and Curses
England: History of a Nation
Royalist, But: Herefordshire in the English Civil War

Auld Enemies
The Scots and the English

David Ross

Illustrated by Rupert Besley

BIRLINN

This new edition first
published in Great Britain in 2012 by
Birlinn Ltd
West Newington House
10 Newington Road
Edinburgh
EH9 1QS

www.birlinn.co.uk

ISBN: 978 1 78027 049 4

British Library Cataloguing-in-Publication Data
A catalogue record for this book is available
on request from the British Library

Typeset by Mark Blackadder

Printed and bound in Britain by Clays Ltd, St Ives plc

Scotland is not wholly surrounded by the sea – unfortunately.
Hugh MacDiarmid, 'The Sea', in *Scottish Scene*

It is very rare to find a foreigner, other than an American, who can distinguish between English and Scots.
George Orwell, *The Lion and the Unicorn*

The fact is, there is no such thing as national character.

There are, however, plenty of stupid prejudices masquerading as scholarly enquiry into how and why we are different from the English.
James Murphy, in *The Herald*, 1992

The Englishman and the Scot have long served as one another's alter ego.
Karl Miller, *Doubles*

What ethic river is this wondrous Tweed
Whose one bank vertue, other vice doth breed?
Andrew Marvell, *The Loyal Scot*

What is clear is that since devolution the English and Scots are drifting further apart and growing more ignorant of each other.
Institute for Public & Political
Research (North), Newcastle, 2008

Contents

An Exploration

The Scots and the English have been neighbour-nations for almost a thousand years. That's a long time in which to get acquainted, and to understand each other. But still today, there is plenty of evidence that despite those ten centuries, much intermingling, and a shared language, the Scots and the English are still something of a mystery to one another. Some observers suggest the mutual ignorance is growing. This book looks into that zone of mystery. It's not about devolution, independence or politics – its raw material lies in the many things the Scots and English have said and written about each other, particularly of a humorous nature, though the humour

can be sharp and bitter at times. The relationship has embraced bloody battles, commercial rivalries, treaties of perpetual friendship made only to be broken, invasions, dynastic links, influences both intended and accidental; and a host of personal connections through many generations. Reaching back into time, drawing on writing, memoirs, conversational remarks, jokes and insults, a complex and many-layered relationship is unpicked. It's a kind of exploration, across one of the oldest unchanged frontiers in Europe. England and Scotland have coexisted as might a dog and a cat in the same household: the one much larger and stronger, sure of its place and willing to be benevolent as long as its supremacy is not challenged, yet puzzled and daunted by the other's scratchy fierceness and complete refusal to assume the secondary role that its smaller size seems to imply. The Scots have always had to explain themselves to the world, and never been reticent about doing so; the English have explained everybody else to their own satisfaction, but kept themselves a mystery.

Things are Speeding up

Between 1707 and 1999 many aspects of the Union between Scotland and England changed. But there was also a solid stability in the political relationship. There was just one Parliament – for much of the time known not merely as the British, but the Imperial Parliament. This did not mean that the two nations coalesced into one. If anything, during the Victorian era (encouraged by the Queen herself) a whole new kind of Scottishness was fashioned, based on aspects of the picturesque past, while in England, the trend was to discard old ways and old styles. In recent years, however, the existence of a Scottish Parliament has set real events in motion. The clever people who planned the Parliament's structure took great care to ensure a voting system that allowed representation

of minority parties and would not ensure a permanent majority for the Labour Party. They should have remembered that Scotland is home of the phrase about best laid plans ganging aft agley (Robert Burns was second only to William Shakespeare as a coiner of remarks destined to become clichés). Labour confidently expected that it would remain the largest and dominant party. Within seven years the Scottish National Party had taken that position, and in only another four it achieved the supposedly impossible, an absolute majority of seats at Holyrood.

Future developments are impossible to forecast, and no direct concern of this book. But what can't be ignored is that since 1999 the relationship between Scotland and England has acquired a new sort of dynamism. Significant differences have opened up. Scotland's policies on care for the aged, on the National Health Service, on bridge tolls and on university fees are all markedly different from England's. Any increase in the powers at the disposal of the Holyrood Parliament is likely to widen the gap. These are all domestic issues. But, if a referendum on staying within the EU should result in an English majority against, and a Scottish majority for, external relations would become a vital issue. Or in another scenario, if Scotland resumed full political independence, what would be the status of the treaties negotiated by the United Kingdom – including its membership of the European Union? Would England and Scotland have to reapply, separately?

A funny thing is, it's all so private. No other nation gives a hoot. The only international bodies who take an interest in Scottish separation are those sporting ones who would prefer to see it ended and have only a single 'British' side, and therefore only one vote, in their deliberations. Scotland and England field separate teams for the Commonwealth Games, but not for the Olympics (had the Olympics been invented in these islands, it would be another story).

Changing Perceptions

The shape of the island of Great Britain probably has something to do with it: the border is narrow compared to the length of both countries. Had the divide run north–south, there would have been far more scope for assimilation (or maybe not: perhaps Celtic-speaking people glaring across barbed wire at English or Danish speakers on the other side). Geologists like to point out that Scotland and England were

once two quite separate land-masses, within the vast primeval Iapetus Ocean, and did not drift into union until around 450 million years ago. Perhaps, in another couple of hundred million years, they will separate again.

The last time a full sense of 'Britishness' existed was between 1939 and 1945, when the struggle to survive and fight for victory took precedence over everything else. But two generations have grown up and reached voting age in post-war Britain. For most electors in England and Scotland, World War II is not even a memory. It is very noticeable that the 'discourse' on Scotland's future – in Scotland – has moved on in the past ten years. From complaint about the Union's failure to take in Scottish aspirations and opinions, it now openly considers how an independent, or semi-independent Scotland could exist in the world. Many people in England would break

the treaty which makes the United Kingdom part of the European Union, while resisting 'with every fibre' (to quote Prime Minister David Cameron) the dissolution of the Treaty of Union made in 1707. For Scotland's young voters, political detachment from England is already obvious and important because it affects their lives. For England's young voters, the notion of political detachment from Scotland has little importance at present, though this may change. The Scottish First Minister got some stick in 2007 and 2011 for the apparently flippant remark that he would like to see a self-governing England. Some English people might like that too, though not all: the journalist Madeleine Bunting wrote, 'I dread the small shorn-ness of England' (*Guardian*).

If Great Britain were a shared beach towel, on a typically

windswept North Sea strand, Scotland was the partner on the outer edge, the windward side, entitled to some of the towel but not too much. Each occupant took the other's presence for granted. Both were equally prepared to get up off their red-white-and-blue towel to shove off anyone who planted themselves too near. Now, it seems to England that Scotland is edging off, on to a towel of its own, perhaps a little more sheltered from the wind, perhaps even provided with little windbreaks that England does not have. The fulcrum has moved, the balance is tipped.

But how different are the Scots and the English, anyway?

Theories, 1.
No Scots, No English – Just Brits

When Julius Caesar's ships came to the coast of Kent, fifty-five years before the beginning of the Common Era, all the inhabitants of the largest island of the British archipelago spoke essentially the same language, Brythonic. Possibly other tongues, older and unrelated, were also used in certain areas, but from north to south, Brythonic was the common speech, no doubt with local variations. It was a 'Celtic' language (indeed it is only in language terms that the word 'Celtic' has any meaning). The inhabitants went in for body decoration; as an old student song has it:

> Ancient Briton never hit on
> anything as good as woad to fit on

but were divided politically into tribal groups. Some may have been descendants of people who had lived there since the last Ice Age, a few thousand years before; others had crossed over recently from the European continent. The Romans noted their tribal names (perhaps gave these names in some cases), but also knew them all as Britons. There were no Scots, and no English, and for that matter no Welsh, though the adjacent, next-largest island, Hibernia, was inhabited by people who might plausibly be referred to as Irish, though some at least would call themselves Scots.

New arrivals and new names reshaped the identities of

Britannia's inhabitants. Scots crossed over from Hibernia, and eventually the wider population assumed their tribal name. Further south, as Roman imperial power collapsed, mercenaries, settlers, and colonists began to arrive from the continent. Two of these north European groups were known to their neighbours as Angles and Saxons; and though the Angles gave their name to the new country, the Saxons were not forgotten, or there would be no Sassenachs. Had certain events gone otherwise, South Norwegians and Western Danes might now be comparing their differences, instead of Scots and English.

Was there genocide or inter-mingling? What the new arrivals did to the earlier inhabitants has long been argued over by historians, archaeologists and linguists. Much more recently, the debate has been joined by genetic scientists, linking our DNA with ancient groups in areas as disparate as the Pyrenees and the Near East. Muscling in on other disciplines, one Oxford geneticist has suggested that a primitive form of Old English was spoken long before the time of the 'Anglo-Saxon' arrivals. Traditional historians tend to treat such intervention as irrelevant, and emphasise the role of culture and environment in the development of national qualities. The show will run and run. In all that follows, though, it is important to remember that whatever the differences in national character, there are no racially 'pure' Scots or English: both have, in the words of the novelist William McIlvanney, a mongrel inheritance.

Theories, 2.
Different Mind-sets?

The English mind has a tendency to be pragmatic and to think in terms of what is real and actual. The Scottish mind has a tendency to be abstract and to think in terms of what can be proved by reasoning. Many, perhaps most, people would agree with this generalisation. In the early 19th century, Sydney Smith gave a fine example of Scottish thinking: 'I overheard a young lady of my acquaintance, at a dance in Edinburgh, exclaim, in a sudden pause of the music, "What you say, my Lord, is very true of love in the *aibstract*, but –" here the fiddlers began fiddling furiously, and the rest was lost.' To put it another way, English thinking works inductively: based on prediction or inference made from regular and sustained observation, as in 'Rain before seven, fine before eleven'. David Hume wondered whether induction was a process of reasoning at all. In Scotland, when directed to serious or intellectual affairs, thought is deductive – it moves towards a conclusion or inference derived from certain premises. If the premises are true, a conclusion drawn from them cannot be false. Even if the premises are false, the process itself is always valid. As the poet Alastair Reid observed, a casual remark about a fine day can be answered by, 'We'll pay for it.'

Henry Thomas Buckle (1821–62), a Londoner, a pioneer of 'scientific history', which looked for basic laws underlying human and national activity, embarked on a vast 'History of

Civilization' but never got beyond the first two volumes, ostensibly on English Civilisation, but much more about France, Spain and Scotland. Buckle was one who argued that the Scots held to a deductive style of reasoning, and thought it related to their religious beliefs. Even when the eighteenth century witnessed a revolutionary development of intellectual life in Scotland, he claimed that this deductive mode limited the benefits of progressive thought. In England, by contrast, the inductive style of thought clarified and passed on by Francis Bacon had eroded the influence of the clergy and largely accounted for English progress. Buckle's general approach to history has been discredited, but the suggestion of different thought-processes is interesting. Sympathetic mutual understanding would not necessarily happen.

This bi-polarity would account for the English being a more conservative people than the Scots. The difference between the law of the two nations may also be a reflection of it: Scottish law, following the continental and old Roman approach, is based on precepts and principles; in England the common law is based on cases and precedents.

Theories, 3.
The Evolution of the Tribe

Sir Arthur Keith (1866–1955) was an eminent Scottish scientist, anatomist and palaeontologist. A keen follower of Charles Darwin, he published *Ethics and Evolution* in 1948. In this book he suggests that evolution was not just a physiological process but a social one, and that an ancient, basic evolutionary drive has formed human communities and still underpins them. He saw it as a natural force which works through us to protect, preserve and enlarge the tribal community against rival groups (*all* other groups are rivals), by violence if necessary. Arguing against scientists who claimed that humanity was intrinsically an ethical species, he believed that at a basic level, the only good that matters to us is the survival of the tribe. For Keith, the role of the politician was to understand this process and work to avoid its bloody, and at worst genocidal, implications. Seeing 'disruption' as natural, if not necessarily desirable, he said in 1919, '… the nearer the blood relationship between two adjacent peoples, the more likely is disruption to occur'.

The old self-awareness of the Scottish people as 'the community of the realm' expressed in the Arbroath Declaration of 1320, and the continuing stalwart refusal to merge Scottish identity with that of the larger adjacent group, come to mind (a thought reflected by the poet Edwin Muir: 'We were a family, a tribe, a people'). Keith's theory can be contested, but it is certainly thought-provoking in any examination of why the Scots and English remain 'different' from one another. The Scottish tribe, officially at least, proclaims itself as wide-open. The term 'affinity Scot' was coined to describe non-Scots with an ancestral or emotional link to Scotland – the English are by no means excluded – who might be persuaded to visit Scotland and spend money. The most hopeful estimate of the size of this 'diaspora' is 100 million people. There is no affinity-English equivalent. Is England one tribe, or several? Keith also noted that 'In England itself the sense of nationality is usually dormant; only an insult or a threat from without stirs this gigantic force into life … it dozes quietly on the hob. Nevertheless English nationality is a force which pervades the whole population lying between Berwick-on-Tweed and Land's End.'

Incidentally, the word 'Scot' has the advantage of not being gender-specific. There is no unisex word for 'person of English origin': is this just happenstance, or another example of different self-perceptions?

Some Current
Cross-Border Thoughts

Yes, Scots are racist, but only to the English ... a nation sunk in corruption, a sense of inadequacy, and above all, a chippy jealousy of its bigger, richer, more outgoing neighbour ... They can then have a high old time up there, sitting around the peat fires, sipping their whisky and all hating the English together; but however much they do it, it will never make them so happy, wealthy or wise as the folk south of Hadrian's Wall.

Simon Heffer, in the *Daily Mail*, September 2002.
The newspaper's Scottish edition did not carry this article.

 I believe passionately in English independence ... I think the English are well capable of self-government and should be given the opportunity.

Alex Salmond, 16 January 2007

I am Scottish and I grew up believing that English and Scottish brought out the best in one another ... I find it easy to be both Scottish and British, happily dualistic.

Andrew O'Hagan, *Daily Telegraph*, 9 December 2007

I will campaign to keep our United Kingdom together with every single fibre that I have.

David Cameron, 6 May 2011

When I was about eight, I informed my parents that I felt more British than Scottish. They were horrified. These days, I feel a lot more Scottish than British. Sometimes I feel more European than British.

Iain Banks, in the *Guardian*, 28 August 2011

And in the meantime what about Britain? The Britain I grew up in: the Britain of the BBC, of manufacturing, of university education, of council housing, civic theatres and libraries? That Britain has been torn up by successive Westminster governments that have pandered with increasing desperation to a middle England that seems determined to live in a low-tax, high-inequality, American-style future. I don't want to live in America. I don't want to live in Thatcherland.

David Greig, in the *Guardian*, 28 August 2011

Guy Lodge, the institute's senior research fellow, said: 'During a time when there is so much debate about the future relationship between England and Scotland, what is clear is that since devolution the English and Scots are drifting further apart and growing more ignorant of each other.'

Institute for Public & Political Research (North), quoted in the *Herald*, 9 June 2008

Getting to Know Each Other

Scotland became a unified kingdom in 1034. England's identity stems from the Norman Conquest of 1066. At certain times before that, it had seemed possible that the Scottish realm would extend as far as the Humber, taking in all of Northumbria and Cumbria. Such a division of the island – Wales apart – would have created two states of comparable size, and led to a history that might have been very different. As it was, the fixing of a frontier from the Solway to the Tweed confirmed an unequal relationship. Scotland was going to have to live with the fact that England was bigger, more populous, and richer. England was also in the way. Sea-lanes to north, east and south-west were open to the Scots, but the land-route south towards the rest of Europe was blocked. The resulting rivalry was well-known on the continent, even rating a line in Dante's *Divine Comedy*. In 'Paradiso' the poet comments: 'There shall be seen that pride that quickens thirst, that makes the Scot and the Englishman mad, so that neither can keep within his own bounds.'

For seven hundred years, successive English kings and governments would make use of their geographical position and their wealth to keep the northern kingdom isolated. As a result, Scotland was poorer than it might have been, but also more dangerous and violent as a neighbour. The English maintained the hope of absorbing Scotland into their own realm, or at least of reducing it to a form of tributary status, in which it could do no harm. For long periods of time, they were able to carry on a national life as if Scotland did not exist – something never possible in reverse. Scotland was a curiosity – a strange, somewhat archaic land known to have its own internal complexities of society, custom and language. A fellow-nation in western Christendom it might be, but to those who lived south of the Humber, Scotland was hardly better known than Lithuania – except for one thing. It alone could invade over land. The Scots had nuisance-value for government, and scare-value for individuals, especially those living north of the Humber.

While Scotland could not reasonably hope to overrun and conquer England, it certainly had the power to inflict heavy damage. Furthermore, from an early stage in national history, the Scots made a bond with England's other neighbours, the French. In official and unofficial concert with the Gaels of Ireland, the Scots also helped to delay the full English

conquest of that country for centuries (though they had a go themselves in the 14th century). Never once until 1603 did the Scots form any sort of military alliance with the English. Indeed, when the young King James I, an involuntary guest of the English Henry V, was taken on campaign in France in the early 1400s, he found himself facing the army of his own countrymen. It had been sent, in his name, by the government of Scotland to help the French against the English. To England, the continuing independence of Scotland was a threat and a distraction.

Even in 1603, when James VI, great-great-grandson of Henry VII of England (and of fifteen other persons including French, Burgundians and a few Scots), achieved his long-awaited status as James I of England, his native country remained a poor relation. Ironically, having got the Scots' king, the English no longer wanted the Scots' territory. The sting had been drawn from the north, they believed, and they thought that Scotland would be a drain on England's wealth. Political union between the two countries was finally brought about, in controversial circumstances, in 1707. This did not mark the end of hostilities, either. Slightly less than forty years later, an army of Jacobite Highlanders invaded England and got to within 120 miles of London.

The battle of Culloden in 1746, fought not between Scots and English, but between Jacobites and Hanoverians (with many Scots among the latter), marks the end of large-scale armed conflict as a means of resolving political differences within the island of Great Britain. Since then, the inhabitants have increasingly followed a 'British' way of life, in their own Scottish, Welsh or English manner. In the eighteenth and nineteenth centuries, many Scots were content to describe themselves as English. Scotland's greatest philosopher, David Hume, was one of these, for a time at least. Later he changed his mind, and wrote to his friend Gilbert Elliot:

I do not believe there is one Englishman in fifty, who, if he heard that I had broke my Neck to night, would not be rejoic'd with it. Some hate me because I am not a Tory, some because I am not a Whig, some because I am not a Christian, and all because I am a Scotsman. Can you seriously talk of my continuing an Englishman? Am I, or are you, an Englishman? Will they allow us to be so? Do they not treat with Derision our Pretension to that Name, and with Hatred our just Pretension to surpass & govern them? I am a citizen of the World, but if I were to adopt any country, it would be that in which I live at present ... [That country was France].

At the time Hume wrote, 1764, a Scotsman, Lord Bute, was the king's chief adviser and had been prime minister until the previous year. It was still a novelty to have a Scot in a leading position in the British state: but this was the moment when the jokes about Scots ruling the English began. Some people tried to promote the term 'British', to the outrage of such populist English politicians as John Wilkes  (1725–97), who saw it as a 'melting-down' of Englishness, and whose whipping-up of anti-Scottish prejudice was furiously denounced in Scotland. One Scot, admittedly a lunatic, tried to assassinate him.

But because Britishness is still an outer layer of identity, felt in the mind rather than in the heart, the old attitudes and rivalries, formed in a very different context, remain, although they are normally expressed in a very much tamer and more playful form nowadays. Even during the Second World War, local attitudes often prevailed. The story is told of a fishing boat from a Buchan port, which happened to be at Lowestoft in June 1940, when the call went out for all available vessels to help in bringing the retreating British army back across the Channel from Dunkirk. Taking his boat inshore through shot and shell, as close as he could get, and surveying the milling troops on the shore and in the water, the skipper bellowed: 'Onybody here fae Peterheid or the Broch?'

The mass of English people did not know the Scots very well until the mid-eighteenth century. They knew the Welsh better, and there are more jokes and rude stories in old English chap-books about Taffy than there are about Sawney. They knew the Irish better too, and once again Irish jokes precede and greatly outnumber jokes about Scots in the early eighteenth century. But by the end of that century a stereotyped English view of the Scots was firmly in place. However much of a distortion it was, an individual personality emerged, cautious with money, curious of accent, logical-minded to the point of perversity. A favourite tale was of the Aberdonian who found a crutch lying in the street, took it home and broke his wife's leg. The Scots did not have a similar caricature of the English. This was partly because the English displayed such variety, from blunt-spoken northerners to their phlegmatic southern country-folk and effervescent Cockneys. As the Scottish writer and politician Christopher Harvie remarks: '"Englishness" has always been notoriously hard to define – definitions, anyhow, are not the sort of thing chaps go in for' (from *Travelling Scot*). But there was another reason. The Scots saw the English less in individual terms than as a mass, a vast group, made up of disparate elements and united in only one thing – they were the other side, the opposition, the 'Auld Enemy'.

What is an Anglo-Scot?

In one of the 16th-century contests of poetic vituperation known as flytings, Walter Kennedy observes of William Dunbar (who came from Lothian):

> In Ingland, owle, suld be thyne habitacione,
> Homage to Edward Langshankis maid thy kyn.
> [You owl, you should be living in England; your forebears paid homage to Edward Longshanks.]

Mockery of the Anglo-Scot goes a long way back. Once this term was used for Scots who went too far in assimilating themselves to an English style – and were regarded as renegades who had repudiated the ways of their own land. Anglo-Scots were seen as Scottish folk for whom Scotland – and so all other Scots – was not good enough. There were few extenuating circumstances. Anglo-Scot could simply mean a person with good reason to feel both Scottish and English, but the term has long been a loaded one. In Scottish usage it implies, maybe not so strongly as in earlier years, someone who has adopted a superior attitude, tone and accent, modelled on English practice, but who does not hesitate to wield some of the symbols of Scottishness, tartan and tweed, country dancing and deer-stalking.

It is said that a Scotchman returning home after some years' residence in England, being asked what he thought of the English, answered: 'They hanna ower muckle sense, but they are an unco braw people to live amang;' which would be a very good story, if it were not rendered apocryphal, by the incredible circumstance of the Scotchman going back.

Thomas Love Peacock (1785–1866), *Crotchet Castle*

… we do not rate highly the Scotsman who has succeeded in becoming an Englishman, unless his Rugby is exceptionally good.

James Bridie (1888–1951), *One Way of Living*

Torquils, Jamies and Fionas turn tartan at the right season, roughly coinciding with the annual northward migration of the royals.

Christopher Harvie, *Travelling Scot* (1999)

The most outspoken critic of the Anglo-Scot was the poet Hugh MacDiarmid, who in one fine raking sweep condemned: '… the whole gang of high mucky-mucks, famous fatheads, old wives of both sexes, stuffed shirts, hollow men with headpieces stuffed with straw, bird-wits, lookers-under-beds, trained seals, creeping Jesuses, Scots Wha Ha'evers, village idiots, policemen, leaders of white-mouse factions and noted connoisseurs of bread and butter … and all the touts and toadies and lickspittles of the English Ascendancy, and their infernal womenfolk, and all their skunkoil skulduggery.' (*Lucky Poet*)

Scottish institutions bolstered Anglo-Scottishness, notably the handful of boarding schools: 'The Scottish public schools have often enough and justifiably enough been seen as an alien element – the fifth column of England', wrote Allan Massie, himself a product of one of them, in 1977. The Scottish Episcopal Church, an integral part of the world-wide Anglican Communion, had natural links with England and was often perceived as the spiritual home of the Anglo-Scots, despite the fact that many of its adherents and clergy had none of the 'superiority' attributes.

Outside Scotland, Anglo-Scots would be indetectable most of the time, taken as English, blending in at the appropriate level of a society more stratified than that of Scotland, except perhaps if they choose to celebrate November 30 and January 25, and Hogmanay. There is no name for an English person who – in England – assumes a Scottish attitude, tone and accent. The breed is too rare, if it exists at all.

More recently, Anglo-Scot might also refer to someone from England who now lives in Scotland and has taken some trouble to learn and adjust to the local customs and practices. This is altogether a kinder usage.

The English in Scotland

In the 1980s the word Anglocracy was coined to suggest the presence of an English élite in control of many aspects of Scottish life. Anglocrats helped to create 'a colonial atmosphere'. The term did not catch on, but there are still complaints when an English person is appointed to some

HAME,
SWEET
SECOND
HAME

senior post in Scotland. Paradoxically, there is pride felt when a Scot, or even an Anglo-Scot, attains some high position in London. But that is put down to individual merit, whereas north of the Border, suspicions arise that the Englishness of a candidate is a trump card. Despite the many Scots in high posts in England, there are few complaints about a Caledocracy.

Since the late 1990s, the number of migrants from England into Scotland has been greater than the number of Scottish migrants into England, reversing a centuries-old trend. The English are the largest minority group in Scotland's population, around 10 per cent of the total. They are not evenly distributed: from the 2001 census it was reckoned that the Borders had the highest proportion of English-born residents, at 16.8 per cent, followed by Dumfries & Galloway, 15.6 per cent, and the Highlands, 13.7 per cent. The lowest proportion was in Glasgow. In 2004 three Stirling University researchers, McIntosh, Sim and Robertson, published a paper in the journal *Sociology*, entitled 'We Hate the English, Except for You, 'cos You're Our Pal'. This attitude was held to be typical: a generalised prejudice that dissolves in the real situations of individual relationships. But even if few interviewees felt they were facing up to 'a belligerent and discriminatory anti-Englishness', many felt they were always seen as different: 'they naturally assume I'm just passing through' was a typical comment. The ear for accent is always acute, and anyone who does not sound Scottish is liable to be asked 'How long are you here for?' This can become irritating after a decade or so.

Yet what many incomers to Scotland appreciate is the sense of a national community, and it is natural in a community to notice, and even be wary of, outsiders. New residents have to put up with that. But a real community is built on shared values and not on ways of speech, and both the natives and the newcomers need to remember this.

The Scots in England

'How long are you here for?' is not asked of Scots in England. Estimates of their number run from two to five million or more, with around 400,000 in London. Few nations celebrate Scottish occasions more enthusiastically than the English. In the remotest parts, people attend Burns Suppers, where they enjoy haggis, toast 'The Lasses', and enthusiastically join hands to sing 'Auld Lang Syne'. Just over three weeks before, they probably sang the same song at a New Year party. Invitations to a St Andrew's Day dinner are gladly received. Almost always, a piper can be found, and in any town of reasonable size, English people will gather to perform Highland reels and other Scottish dances. (By contrast, an English person who set out to celebrate St George's Day in Scotland would be accused of cultural imperialism and gross disrespect for local sensitivities.) This is less the achievement of English-dwelling Scots than the embracing, by the natives, of a chance to enjoy themselves. For this is a deep secret of the English – that they like to escape from their Englishness occasionally. But all this took time to happen.

John Mair (sometimes Latinised as Major, 1467–1550) was a Scottish scholar with an international career and reputation. In 1521 his Latin treatise, *A History of Greater Britain, both England and Scotland*, was published, with the famous passage:

It would be to the utmost advantage to both kingdoms

that they should be under the rule of one monarch, who should be called King of Britain, always provided he had a just and honourable title to it … I pray to God, the Ruler of all, that He may grant such a peace to the Britons that one of their kings in a marriage union may by just title possess both kingdoms.

Mair lived at a time when warfare between Scotland and England was not a memory but a reality. British unity then, like European unity now, seemed a way to exchange warfare for peace and prosperity.

It was with the arrival of their new king, James I, from Edinburgh in 1603, that the English first got to know the Scots as something other than an armed and hostile force. Soon there were complaints about the newcomers:

They beg our lands, our goods, our lives,
They switch our nobles, and lye with their wives;
They pinch our gentry, and send for our benchers,
They stab our sergeants and pistoll our fencers.
– from an anonymous English comment of the period.

For King James, the death of his distant relative Elizabeth I of England provided the opportunity he had long and impatiently awaited – to become king of England (and Ireland) as well as of Scotland. He was over the moon, and very soon over the Border; but many of his Scottish subjects were less enthusiastic about his transition. One of them, William Forbes of Disblair, wrote *A Pil for Pork-Eaters: Or, A Scots Lancet for an English Swelling*:

CURS'D be the Day (for then we were betray'd)
When first our King the English Scepter sway'd.
As never State nor Kingdom did before:

> From neighbouring States we no Assistance crav'd,
> We scorn'd by foreign Yokes to be enslav'd;
> Had Wealth at Home, Alliances Abroad;
> Yea of our Friendship France itself was proud;
> Each Scot was brave, with Noble Courage fir'd;
> Our Court Polite, and every where admir'd.
> Thus from a Nation full of Power and Fame,
> We're dwindl'd to a Thing, scarce worth a Name.

Dissatisfaction in Scotland was so great that James had an Act of Parliament passed in 1609 against 'Scandalous Speeches and Libels', forbidding the Scots to insult the English in: '… pasquillis, libellis, rymis, Cockalanis, comedies and sicklyk occasionis whereby they slander maligne and revile the estait and country of England and divers his majesties honorable Counsallors, magistratis and worthie subjects of that his majesties kingdome'. Imprisonment, banishment, fines and 'mair rigorous Corporal pane' were all threatened against those who persisted in such un-British behaviour.

Numerous Scots came south to join the court, and the invasion, though on a small scale compared with the next century, was not always well received. In 1605 three playwrights, George Chapman, Ben Jonson and John Marston were briefly imprisoned for a rude reference to Scots in their play *Eastward Ho*. One character, Seagull, refers to the colony of Virginia as an agreeable place without any unpleasant inhabitants, except for 'a few industrious Scots perhaps, who are indeed dispersed over the face of the whole earth. But as for them there are no greater friends to England and Englishmen, when they are on't, in the world than they are. And for my own part, I would that a hundred thousand of them were there, for we are all one countrymen now, ye know, and we should find ten times more comfort of them there than we do here.'

In the summer of 1618 a Scot, Thomas Ross, fixed a document to the door of St Mary's Church, Oxford. Written in Latin, the text (now lost) recommended that all Scotsmen resident in England, with the exception of the king, his son, and a very few others, should be sent back to their homeland. This proposal for repatriation became notorious, and Ross was sent back to Scotland himself, to be tried by the High Court in Edinburgh – although he had committed no offence in Scotland – for his 'villainous and infamous Pasquell or Thesis, and damnable appendices subjoined thairto'. Without being able to read the original, we cannot know whether the author's intention was satirical in some way, or whether he felt that his fellow-expatriates should be sent home to be safe from the fleshpots of England, or that they ought to be concerning themselves with the affairs of their own country. Perhaps to his surprise, he was sentenced to have his right hand cut off, followed by his head. On 10 September 1618 the execution duly took place; his head was put on a spike at the Netherbow, and his hand at the West Port, of Edinburgh.

In 1700, during futile negotiations on a possible union, the English Sir Edward Seymour remarked that Scotland 'was a beggar, and whoever married a beggar could only expect a louse for a portion'. The anonymous Scottish writer of *The True Scottish Genius* in 1704 described his country as:

Bereav'd of Power, of Riches, and of Trade,
Still slavishly to England's Int'rest ty'd.

The influx of Scots to England, especially London, was much greater in the eighteenth century, and noted by satirical writers, as in this anonymous verse:

See how they press to cross the Tweed,
And strain their limbs with eager speed!

While Scotland from her fertile shore
Cries, 'On my sons, return no more.'
Hither they race with willing mind,
Nor cast one longing look behind.

Lord Bute
wondering why nobody
likes him

In the 1760s, a Scottish peer, Lord Bute, became prime
minister. He owed the position to the fact that he was a
favourite of King George III – something that did not endear
him to the many English who thought, in the words of one
of their later versifiers that 'King George the Third Ought
never to have occurred'. The anti-Scottish publication *The
North Briton* objected to Bute on principle:

> The first is, that he is a Scot … I am certain, that reason
> could never believe that a Scot was fit to have
> management of English affairs … A Scot hath no more
> right to preferment in England than a Hanoverian or a
> Hottentot.

They also objected to his finding positions and sinecures for other Scots. In 1762 an anonymous diatribe entitled *A British Antidote to Caledonian Poison* appeared, satirising the Scottish influx and Bute's jobs-for-the-boys:

> Sister Peg, our ancient friend
> Sends Macs and Donalds without end.

This, incidentally, seems to be the earliest reference to Scots as 'Macs'. A braver poet, Charles Churchill (1731–64) put his name to *The Prophecy of Famine*, a satirical poem on the Scottish influx. It mocks the Scots' pretension to being all of noble blood, like his shepherd-boy heroes, Jocky and Sawney, 'Whose birth beyond all question springs/From great and glorious, though forgotten, kings.' Another Scots boast, that the Romans had never conquered their country, was also dealt with; Famine, the foster-mother of all Scots, is made to say:

> Lang free, because the race of Roman braves
> Thought it not worth their while to make us slaves.

Churchill dealt briskly with the many Scottish poets and writers who descended on London:

> These simple bards, by simple prudence taught,
> To this wise town by simple patrons brought,
> In simple manner utter simple lays,
> And take, with simple pensions, simple praise.
> For these Scots, England awaits:
> For us, the Earth shall bring forth her increase,
> For us, the Flocks shall wear a Golden Fleece;
> For Beeves shall yield us dainties not our own,
> And the Grape shall bleed a nectar yet unknown,

> For our advantage shall their Harvests grow,
> And Scotsmen reap, what they disdained to sow.

But many others apart from poets came down. To cite just one example, Henry Brougham, born in Edinburgh in 1778, settled in London in 1805, learned English law, campaigned against slavery, became lord chancellor in 1830 and was responsible for the forming of the Central Criminal Court, county courts, the founding of the Society for the Diffusion of Useful Knowledge, and the establishment of London University. He also played a leading part in the reform of Parliament and the electoral system. Self-important, domineering, jealous of others' success, ready to betray anyone or anything for his own cause, or even his own gratification, Brougham's contribution to English – and British – life is very great, but he was only one of many Scots who came south, learned at least some of the rules of the English game of life, and did well for themselves. In 1917, the Anglo-Scottish author Ian Hay made a playful comment in a book written for Americans and entitled *The Oppressed English*: 'Today a Scot is leading the British Army in France, another is commanding the British Grand Fleet at sea, while a third directs the Imperial General Staff at home. The Lord Chancellor is a Scot; so are the Chancellor of the Exchequer and the Foreign Secretary … Yet no one has ever brought in a bill to give home rule to England!' Similar comments have often been made in later decades.

A young Scottish civil servant, working in St Andrew's House in Edinburgh, was sent down to London to represent his department at a number of meetings. It was his first visit to Whitehall. When he returned to Edinburgh, his colleagues quizzed him about his experiences.

'And what did you think about the English?' asked one, eventually.

'The English? I never met any,' said the young man. 'I only spoke to Heads of Departments.'

For two centuries, a leavening of Scots, usually in the professional classes, has been accepted as part of English life. Unsurprisingly, the great majority of England-dwelling Scots keep a sense of commitment to the United Kingdom with its London Parliament. They like to feel they are something other than *Gastarbeiter* or economic migrants among the English – British fellow-citizens with a common loyalty and shared values. They don't hide their Scottishness, and tune it up a bit at Burns Suppers where some of the Caledonian mystique can be kindly explained to the appreciative locals. But their Scotland is a place of nostalgia and highly selective tradition, and they look with some dismay at the way in which their stay-at-home Scottish compatriots are moving out of the British consensus. If Great Britain was once a playing field where Tories and Labour could kick the same ball from one end to the other (with a few Liberals here and there), it is not like that now. The England-dwelling Scots want Scotland to stay as it was, a kind of Never-Land where nothing changes.

Scots in England

An Awful Truth

Over the years, the Scots have given much thought to the English – much more than the English have given to the Scots. In fact, one of the Scots' beefs against the English is that, most of the time, they don't seem to even notice Scotland is there. In the mid-nineteenth century, the Scottish academic John Stuart Blackie was talking to Dr Benjamin Jowett, of Oxford University.

'I hope you in Oxford don't think we hate you?'

'We don't think about you,' was the reply.

Three hundred years before that, Lord Clarendon had noted that 'when the whole nation was solicitous to know

what passed weekly in Germany and Poland and all other parts of Europe, no man ever enquired what was doing in Scotland, nor had that kingdom a place or mention in one page of any gazette, so little the world heard or thought of that people'.

The same thought was echoed by the Scottish writer Alastair Reid, in a *New Yorker* survey of the Scots, from 1964: 'Of all the grievances nursed by the Scots, none is greater than the fact that the English apparently do not bother to hate back.' In late 2011 an editorial in the London-based *Guardian* commented that 'Most people in England seem serenely unaware of what is happening' in Scotland (discussing the debate on what is variously known as 'devo-max' or 'devolution-lite').

The reason is that they have never felt any particular need to do so. Apart from the much-invaded inhabitants of northern England, for whom 'Scotch' was a dirty word during the Middle Ages, the English had very little knowledge of the country, or need to acquire any. Even in the mid-twentieth century, Trevor Royle, as an English child living in Scotland, noted that his English relatives viewed Scotland as a complete popular stereotype: 'a country of quaint, hairy-kneed and parsimonious old men who went about muttering into their whisky: "It's a braw bricht moonlicht nicht the nicht, ye ken."'

Paradoxically, however, the English have written much more about Scotland and the Scots than the Scots have about England. From the sixteenth century until the twentieth, a succession of English travellers wrote about their impressions of the country to the north, and of its people. A few were filled with hostile prejudice, but most tried to be fair. There are no equivalents from Scotland; those Scots who wrote about life in England had no interest in explaining the idiosyncrasies of the country to their fellow Scots. Perhaps the nearest was the novelist Tobias Smollett in *Roderick Random*, whose hero of

Tobias Smollett

the same name comes from Scotland (like his creator) to experience the quirks and oddities of life in England. Smollett also complained in a letter of 1754 about being tired of 'this Land of Indifference and Phlegm', but he never got tired enough to consider returning to Dunbartonshire. For the English, Scotland was an exotic place, rich in the differences and discomforts which give zest and interest to a travelogue. For the Scots, England did not offer the same opportunities. The amenities of England were too well known to bear description. Its attractions were not found in wild country, uncouth habits, homes and language, but in superior comforts, laden tables, good roads and urbane gatherings at places like Bath. Incoming Scots, mostly from the wealthier or aspiring sections of society, took these things almost instantly for granted, and would never have shown themselves so unsophisticated as to write books about them.

Some Aspects of Englishness

(As perceived, or put about, by the Scots)

Never having understood the English, the Scots have tended to resort to the put-down, picking on the least attractive qualities which they detect.

The Bumptious Englishman

The John Bull-ish heartiness of a certain type of Englishman is something that irks many Scots. They do not see it as genuine openness but as ostentation, or even as a cover for a more sinister attitude. The Englishman's jovial smile is merely a trick to lull you into a false sense of security before he runs off with your property. A modern Gaelic poem sums up this suspicious point of view:

> Cheers!
> The lads arrived one day
> In the pub
> Nattering in Gaelic.
>
> And a big posh Englishman arrived amongst them,
> Full of surprise at their chat,
> And offered them a dram,
> And they accepted it with alacrity,
> And then another,
> And another and another.

And, in parting,
He asked them, perhaps,
To drink his own health
In their own language,
And they raised their glasses
And cried out in Gaelic as one:
Good health, you arsehole!   (From Gaelic)

An older and more subtle example of the same thing comes
from a resort village in Galloway. A jolly English gent and his
family had been coming to the place for several summers, and
felt they knew it and its inhabitants well. As the Englishman
was strolling down the village street one day, he passed one of
the residents, standing by his front door. Close by there was a
fat pig, rootling about in the gutter.

'Morning, Sandy,' called the visitor, then, nodding at the
pig: 'Is that a friend of yours?'

'No, no,' said the native, quietly. 'Just an acquaintance,
same as yourself.'

An even earlier example comes from the seventeenth
century, by which time Scots who had business with the king
came regularly to London. One of these was a tall, burly
Highlander, Sir Robert Bleakie. While in London, he was
invited to a dinner party where there was a mixed gathering of
English and Scots. After the bottle had passed round a few
times, and the spirits of the assembly began to rise, an English
general, a trooper of fame and a noted bon viveur, rose to speak.

'Gentlemen, when I am in my cups, and the wine begins
to warm my blood, I have an absurd custom of railing against
the Scots. Knowing my weakness, I hope no member of the
company will take it amiss.'

Bleakie in turn rose up, and replied, with perfect simplicity
and good nature.

'Gentlemen, I too must confess to a weakness. When I am

in my cups, and the wine warms my blood, if I hear a man rail against the Scotch, I have an absurd custom of immediately kicking him out of the room. Knowing my weakness, I hope no gentleman will take it amiss.'

On that occasion, it was noted that the general did not follow his usual custom. (It must be said that no more is known of Sir Robert; he is probably the product of someone's imagination.)

The English Intellectual

'What is it about the English and intellectuals? ... an English intellectual is either not English or else, if his papers are invincibly in order, not an intellectual ... The English behave as if intellectuals were unicorns: if you see one, you know it isn't one.'

Neal Ascherson, *Games with Shadows* (1988)

In their exchange of letters about the English, published as *A Small Stir*, James Bridie and Moray McLaren enjoyed having a go at that 'most secluded thing, an English intellectual', and the 'thin, high note of sneering denigration which sounds through so much of their able, sometimes brilliant writing'. Highbrow English writers, said Bridie, 'write admirably ... It looks like nonsense. It smells like nonsense. It tastes like nonsense. I believe it is nonsense. But perhaps that is also a characteristic of the English, that they write nonsense really well.'

The intellectual qualities of English and anglicising writers were also assailed by Hugh MacDiarmid in *Gairmscoile*:

Ablachs, and scrats, and dorbels o' a' kinds
Aye'd drob me wi' their puir ell-dronin' minds,

Wee drochlin' craturs drutling their bit thochts
The dorty bodies! Feech! Nae Sassunach drings
'll daunton me.

It was MacDiarmid who described London literary critics as recalling to him 'that extraordinary chirruping conversation which sounds almost human but, on investigation with an electric torch, is found to be merely a couple of hedgehogs courting beneath one's window' (*Lucky Poet*). In England it was, and often still is, considered good form to play down one's intelligence and breadth of cultural awareness – a becoming modesty and courteous acknowledgement that others might not rise to the same level. In Scotland there is less hesitancy. Intelligence has long been the requirement for 'getting on' and therefore has to be displayed. The 'lad o' pairts', encouraged from primary school upwards to extend his knowledge, might be somewhat baffled on coming to England and finding that the conversational level is pitched at a point where his brilliance is hard to display. He might even scent a touch of hypocrisy and would certainly feel comfortably superior.

The Cool Englishman

A definite English characteristic recognised and appreciated by the Scots is coolness or sang-froid, exemplified at the Battle of Waterloo by an exchange between Lord Uxbridge and the Duke of Wellington.

Uxbridge: 'By God, Sir, my leg's been shot off.'

Wellington: 'By God, Sir, so it has.'

A group of English football supporters were drinking quietly in a Glasgow bar, when in came a huge red-haired man wearing a Scotland shirt and a kilt, with his face painted in a blue and white saltire.

'All English skunks get oota here!' he bellowed, and advanced threateningly.

The visitors took one look at him and fled, without waiting to finish their drinks. All except one, who continued to stand calmly at the bar.

'My, there certainly were a lot of them, weren't there!' he said.

A Scot was paying a weekend visit to an English business acquaintance's home. On the first evening, quite by accident, he entered the wrong bathroom and found his host's wife in the bath. Hurriedly retreating, he sought out his host, who was downstairs, and apologetically explained his misadventure.

The Englishman looked up from his newspaper.

'Skinny old thing, isn't she?' he remarked.

The Formal Englishman

The English stiff upper lip is something Scots like to poke fun at. A once popular comic story told of the three Englishmen, survivors of a shipwreck, who were washed up on a desert island. For five years they never exchanged a word, as they had not been introduced to one other. More genuinely, when the writer Gerald Brenan, aged eighteen, walked half-way across Europe with an older friend, John Hope-Johnstone (incidentally of Scottish Border extraction) sleeping in barns, he found 'we had no names by which to call one another. To have used surnames would have seemed too formal whereas Christian names were taboo because they were too intimate. We

therefore addressed each other as "Hullo" or "I say", delivered
in a particular tone.'

The English Club

The clubbish, coded world of Englishness has always been a
mystery to Scots, and even those who joined it, like the writer
John Buchan, never felt entirely at home. One who felt its
combination of insidious charm and alienness was Ralph
Glasser, in his memoir *Gorbals Boy at Oxford*. He is speaking
of his friends James and Bill, 'grown-up school prefects,
descendants of Stalky & Co …' they would always be the
fixers, the cool-headed operators, the secretive network of
power that I would never be permitted to join'. Bill summed
it up for his benefit. 'You're too fundamental for the likes of
us. We are just the operators behind the scenes! We enjoy the
game, that's all. We have no principles, really, except to keep
the status quo – the game as we know it.'

The Mean-Spirited Englishman

There are relatively few Scottish stories about mean Englishmen. Meanness is not seen as a typical English characteristic,
and aggressive humour, with its instinct to go for the exposed
jugular, finds other targets. But an English refusal to accept,
and respect, Scottish customs is bound to attract criticism.

A wealthy English tenant had taken over a Scottish laird's
shooting lodge for the season. Included among the fixtures
and fittings was the resident piper, MacKillop. His function
was to play the bagpipes outside at breakfast-time, and to
come into the dining-room after dinner to play a pibroch.
Between these times he did nothing, and the tenant resented

this. He also resented that each evening the butler placed a tumbler full of malt whisky on the table for MacKillop to consume before he began to play. He calculated that the piper was getting through a bottle of the expensive stuff in a week. One evening he ordered the butler to leave out a glass of water instead of whisky. The water was ignored, and the playing that night was terrible. Even the tenant noticed, and a Scottish neighbour, who was a guest, beckoned to the piper as he paused between tunes and said:

'Something wrong with the pipes tonight, MacKillop?'

'Aye,' said MacKillop. 'Dry. They need whisky, malt whisky.'

His eye was fixed meaningfully on the tenant, who, not wishing to seem mean in front of his guests, asked the butler to provide a glass of whisky. MacKillop downed it in one.

'I thought you said it was for the pipes!' cried the tenant, stung to protest.

'Aye, but it needs blawing into them,' said MacKillop.

The Riotous English

'… rioting is a recurrent English activity with a long history … Rioting is at least as English as thatched cottages and honey still for tea … the traditional resort of those who feel excluded and oppressed by the social and political structure under which – rather than in which – they live.' The writer Neal Ascherson noted this in *Games with Shadows* (1988). It is not necessarily confined to the excluded or deprived, however; the novelist Evelyn Waugh referred to the sound of English county families 'baying for broken glass'.

Ascherson's point seems to be borne out by the events of twenty-three years later in the summer of 2011, when sudden widespread disturbances and looting broke out in English cities. Similar scenes did not happen in Scotland (indeed police from the Strathclyde force were bussed south to help keep order in Birmingham), and the Scottish first minister's comments on this were seen by some English newspapers as 'gloating' over England's misfortunes.

The Ruthless Englishman

Ruthlessness is an English quality held in reserve, like tear gas. It is stowed away, well behind the frontal defences of politeness and understatement, and indeed these perhaps only exist because the English have developed tight lids for their own ferocity. As a result, they were slow to get going in a war, but, after a few setbacks, usually produced men to see it through, however bloodily. 'Whenever I hear of English ruthlessness in some remote place, I always imagine it being expressed (if it can be expressed in words at all) in a homely North of England accent. "You boogers 'ave asked for it, and by goom, you're going to get it." Then, with smiling countenance, the Englishman proceeds to lam into his opponent and destroy him, rules or no rules.' (Moray McLaren, *A Small Stir.*)

Some Aspects of Scottishness

(As perceived or put about by the English)

'… they've got a sort of identity, you know, because
they've got a Scottish sort of heritage about kilts and
bagpipes and all that sort of stuff whereas I mean
England doesn't have that sort of identity really.'

English woman resident in Scotland,
quoted in *Sociology* journal, 2004

The English are sure that they understand the Scots, and their
perceptions of Scottishness are closely linked to certain key-
words, among which are 'canny', 'pawky', 'dour' and 'mean'.
Any sign of a Scot exhibiting these characteristics will be grati-
fying, though some caution may be necessary. As Conan
Doyle makes Sherlock Holmes observe in *The Valley of Fear*:
'You are developing a certain unexpected strain of pawky
humour, Watson, against which I must learn to guard myself.'

The Canny Scot

'Hamish is a canny Scot, he's always saying "I canny do this"
and "I canny do that"' (Graeme Garden and Barry Cryer,
'Hamish and Dougal'.) 'Canny' is an interesting word, one of
numerous Scots terms borrowed into standard English, and
used by the English to describe the Scots when they don't want
to be rude to them. 'Canny Scot' offers a certain friendly but

wary respect for the qualities it implies. No single term corresponds exactly, but they include caution, prudence, shrewdness – but also being knowledgeable, and a bit crafty. It used to be applied quite often to Scottish bankers until it became apparent in recent years that their canniness was limited to their own welfare and rewards.

Three men came along to pay their respects after the death of a friend. They were an Irishman, an Englishman and a Scotsman. As they looked on their former acquaintance in his coffin, the Irishman said:

'He was always generous. He once lent me ten pounds and I never paid it back. Now I will.'

And he took a ten-pound note from his wallet and put it in the coffin.

'He lent me money too,' said the Englishman. 'Twenty pounds – and he never reminded me about it.'

He produced a twenty-pound note and placed it in the coffin.

'And me,' sighed the Scot. 'He lent me fifty pounds, and I never got round to paying it back. But now it's time.'

Bringing out cheque-book and pen, he wrote out a cheque for eighty pounds. Placing it reverently in the coffin, he removed the two bank-notes and put them in his pocket.

Scots can however be too canny for their own good:

'I never get a decent cup of coffee,' sighed Sandy.

'Why is that?'

'Well, when I'm at home, I don't like to put more than one teaspoonful of sugar in, because of the cost. When I'm given coffee by someone else, I always ask for three teaspoonfuls, to make the most of the chance. But I really only like coffee with two sugars.'

Being a financially prudent man, Mr MacPherson was rather upset when he accidentally let a 50p piece fall into the public toilet. What shall I do? he wondered. Is it worth delving in there for 50p? Then he had a brainwave. Reaching into his pocket, he found another 50p piece, and dropped it in too. A pound's another matter entirely, he thought, rolling up his sleeve.

The Informal Scot

A Glaswegian, used to his city's custom of sharing taxis with strangers, was queuing for a taxi at Euston Station, when he heard a man give the driver an address in the same street that he wanted. Quickly moving to the head of the line, he jumped into the same cab. Clasping his suitcase on his knees, he turned to the other passenger and said, pleasantly:

'My name's Buchanan.'

'Mine', said the other, chillily, 'is not.'

The Conceited Scot

To the English, many Scots are far too keen to assert their Scottishness at every turn, along with a tedious listing of the benefits that Scotland has bestowed on the world, from golf and whisky to waterproof cloth and chloroform, and, more recently, cloned sheep. The country of 'Here's tae us – wha's like us?' has got a good conceit of itself. This is potentially a dangerous weakness, of course, and the English have long been aware of it. Complacency comes before a tumble (as the Scottish soccer side has experienced on more than one occasion). The eighteenth-century English writer Anthony Powell noted it in his diatribe *Caledonia*:

Such Mediocrity was ne'er on view,
Bolster'd by tireless Scottish Ballyhoo –
Nay! In two qualities they stand supreme:
Their self-advertisement and their self-esteem.

The people are proud, arrogant, vain-glorious boasters,
bloody, barbarous and inhuman butchers. Couzenage
and theft is in perfection among them, and they are
perfect English-haters, they show their pride in exalting
themselves, and depressing their neighbours.

Thomas Kirke, *A Modern Account of Scotland
by an English Gentleman* (1679)

I should hardly call a Scotchman conceited, though
there is often something that borders strongly on the
appearance of it. He has (speaking in the lump) no
personal or individual pretensions. He is not proud of
himself, but of being a Scotchman.

William Hazlitt (1778–1830), *On the Scotch Character*

On one occasion, a Scot was reciting to an English acquaintance the usual list of Scottish gifts to the world, from the
pneumatic tyre to the mutton pie, when he was interrupted.

'I thought the greatest thing to come out of Scotland was
the M74,' said the Englishman.

The Prickly Scot

A London-dwelling Scot met a friend one day, who noticed
his long face.

'What's the matter, Mungo?'

'Well, I was on jury service, and I was given three days in
jail.'

'For being on a jury? How did that happen?'

'The judge said "What is your name?" and I said "Mungo Hamish MacTaggart." He said "Are you Scottish, by any chance?" and I said "Are you a bloody comedian?"'

The Stingy Scot

Of all accusations and teases levelled at the Scots by the English, this is by far the most frequent, and one of the oldest. Stinginess was an aspect of Scottish canniness when carried too far – or exaggerated for effect. When the English wanted to mock the Scots, this was the readiest handle to reach for.

A man went into a chemist's shop in Aberdeen and left without picking up his change. The chemist tried to attract his attention by knocking on the window with a sponge.

A Scotsman went to the dentist with a raging toothache.

'It will have to come out,' said the dentist.

'What will that cost?' asked the patient.

'Twenty pounds.'

'What will it cost just to loosen it, and I'll pull it out myself?'

A Scotsman by mistake put five pounds into the church plate as the beadle held it out. He beckoned to the beadle, and whispered: 'Can you treat that as a season?'

Englishman: I hear the price of petrol's coming down.
Scotsman: Is that so? What a relief!
Englishman: But you don't own a car.
Scotsman: No, but I have a cigarette-lighter.

A Scotsman with a fine mop of hair went past the barber's window. He saw a notice: 'Haircuts £10. Shaves £2.' He went in, sat down, and said:

'I want my head shaved.'

A Scots laird invited some people to a meal at his castle. They sat down at table in a high, cold room, and were served plates with nothing on them but rather unappetising-looking pieces of bread. For a while they gazed at them, then, when the laird began to eat, they rather unenthusiastically followed his example. After a while the laird's servant came in and, approaching his master, whispered:

'Shall I bring in the hen?'

'No, no,' said the laird. 'Not yet.'

He continued to chew on his somewhat stale bread, and the other guests, heartened by the thought of the hen to come, did likewise. Eventually the servant came in again:

'Is it time for the hen?'

'I'll call you when it is,' said the laird.

At last, when the bread was eaten up, the laird called for his servant, who duly appeared.

'Now bring in the hen,' he said, and the guests sat up expectantly. The servant came in, carrying a live hen in his arms, and set it down on the floor.

'We don't want to waste the crumbs,' said the laird.

The Clever Scot

In the long war of words and wit that has characterised the Scots' relations with the English at least since the thirteenth century, the Scots have been identified at various times as mean, dour, greedy, boastful, gauche, flea-bitten, poverty-stricken, unwashed, drunken and a number of other things. But whatever insults are slung north over the Border, they rarely suggest that the level of intelligence is lower on that side. Perhaps the fact that Scottish emigration to England was mostly a 'brain-drain' has something to do with it. The English can poke fun at the Scots in many ways, but a joke that shows an Englishman outsmarting a Scot would be most unusual. But then, unlike the Scots, the English don't set great store by cleverness. The Lewis-born Tory politician Iain McLeod was criticised by his colleague Lord Salisbury as being 'too clever by half'. Scottish humour makes the most of this.

'How's your brother Donald?'

'Oh, he's never been the same since his accident. They had to remove a third of his brain, you know.'

'Oh dear, where is he, then?'

'We sent him to England. He's doing fine there.'

'Which hospital?'

'Who said anything about a hospital?'

A Scotsman once asked an Englishman if he'd heard the joke about the skull of William Shakespeare, aged twelve, being put on display at Stratford on Avon. 'No,' said the Englishman, 'what is it?'

Scottish jokes about English stupidity are centred on a basic supposition that the English are just not very bright. They don't get the point quickly enough. But sometimes the Englishman's stupidity can rebound on the smart Scots:

Two Scotsmen and an Englishmen were imprisoned in a Middle Eastern jail. After a long time, they unearthed a dirty old lamp in the corner. It proved to be an Aladdin-type lamp complete with genie, who duly offered each of them a wish.

'I wish I was home in Edinburgh,' said the first Scotsman. And he vanished.

'I wish I was home in Glasgow,' said the second, and he too disappeared.

The Englishman scratched his head.

'I don't know if I want to be in London with my mum or in Manchester with my girl-friend,' he said. 'I wish my pals were here to help me decide.'

And, in a flash, they were.

Two cars collided somewhere in the Borders. One was driven by an Englishman, the other by a Scot. They were uninjured, but the damage made it impossible for either to drive away. As they waited for the police to arrive, the Scot produced a bottle of whisky and hospitably offered it first to the Englishman.

'Calms the nerves, after a shake-up like that,' he said.

But when the Englishman handed back the bottle after taking a hefty swig, the Scot put it away without drinking any.

'Aren't you having some too?' asked the Englishman.

'I'll wait until the police have been,' was the answer.

At least one joke brands both sides as equally dumb:

Scotsman: Guess how many ferrets I've got in this bag, and I'll give you both of them.

Englishman: Five?

Scotsman: That's near enough.

Interchangeable Jokes

If an English–Scottish joke can be reversed simply by switching the names around, it's not the genuine article, but one of those all-too-common international jokes that flit around from place to place, impersonal and ineffective. The humorous equivalent of a raspberry, it hardly expresses any feeling and fails to prick the skin.

Tell me one thing that's wrong with England/Scotland?
It's above sea-level.

How do you stop an Englishman/Scotsman jumping into the River Thames/Clyde?
You don't.

You can always tell a Scotsman/Englishman – but you can't tell him much.

'If I had a wish,' sighed the Englishman, 'it would be to build a twenty-foot high wall round the whole of England, to protect it from every kind of foreign influence.'
    'If I had a wish,' said the Scotsman, 'it would be to fill the whole thing with water to the brim.'

History and Myth

One of the oldest jibes cast at the English by the Scots was that England, unlike Scotland, had been a conquered nation. And that not once, but four times – by Romans, Saxons, Danes and Normans:

> For our Heretage was ever Free,
> Since Scota of Aegypt tuik the Sea,
> Whilst ye have ever Conquered been:
> For a Thousand Pounds of Gold schein
> To Julius Caesar payit yee
> Of tribute, thus ye was not free;
> With Saxons syne ye were orthrawn …

In this anonymous poem, the four conquests of England are listed, culminating with:

> A Bastard came out of Normandy,
> Conquest Ingland all hailily.   [entirely]

This war of words was still going strong some three hundred years later, when a Scottish writer, G. Steel, in 1700, during the period of hostility before the Union, invented a dialogue between kings Robert III of Scotland and Henry IV of England, in which the former says:

Thus four times thirled and overhald, [bound and conquered]
You're the great refuse of all the warld.

In the fifteenth century, another anonymous Scot assailed the
English pretension, stemming from Geoffrey of Monmouth
(and with the serious aim of asserting England's primacy
within Britain), that Brutus, 'noblest Roman of them all', was
its founding father. The Scots preferred to parade their own
equally improbable origin from Scota, daughter of a Pharaoh.
At the same time the writer throws a barb at Pope Gregory
the Great's famous reported comment, noted in Bede's 'History of the English Church' and cherished by later Anglo-
Saxon generations, that Anglian slaves in the Roman market
were 'Not Angles, but Angels':

Ye, Inglische hursone, sumtyme will avant [whoreson, boast]
Your progeny from Brutus to haif tane,   [taken]
And sumtyme from ane angell or ane sanct,
As Angelus and Anglus both war ane.

Angellis in erth yit hard I few or nane,   [heard]
Except the feyndis with Lucifer that fell.
Avant you, villane, of that lord allane,
Tak thy progeny from Pluto, prince of Hell.

Because ye use in hoillis to hyd your sell,   [holes]
Anglus is cum from Angulus in deid.
Above all uderis Brutus bure the bell
Quha slew his fader, houping to succeid.
Than chus you ane of thais, I rek not ader: [care]
Tak Beelzebub or Brutus to be your fader.

If it was angels, says the poet, it must have been from the fallen
angels that the English were descended. Anyway, Angle comes

from angulus (a dark corner). And furthermore Brutus killed his own father to speed up his inheritance. Take your pick, I don't mind. According to your own claim, you are either descended from the Devil or from Brutus the parricide.

It was an ancient conceit of the Scots – borrowed from the French according to an eminent scholar – to pretend that the English were born with tails. The legend goes back to a story that an Englishman pinned a tail upon St Augustine, and so his nation was appropriately punished by God, who inflicted tails upon them. In one of the legends of William Wallace, his famous confrontation with the English soldiers in Lanark in 1296 began when he protected a small boy who had put his fingers behind his back and waggled them like a tail at the angry pikemen.

In another of the flytings of Scottish poets in the reign of James IV we find these lines:

Thy forefader maid irisch & irisch men thin
Throu his tresoun broght inglis rumplis in.   [English tails]

A curious reference is made in the anonymous *Voyage of Kynge Edwarde*, describing the English king's invasion of Scotland in 1298, to the abbot of Aberbrothock (Arbroath), who 'made the people of Scotlande beleve theat there was but women and no men in Englande'. Whether the abbot believed that the English nation was half composed of cross-dressing females, or whether he was merely ascribing a certain femininity to Englishmen, akin to the 'mincing Jeremies' gibes of a later time, remains unclear.

Complacent in their possession of an apostle as patron saint, the Scots also dwelt on the dubious origin of England's chosen saint:

To save a maid St George a dragon slew,
A brave exployt if all that's said is true,
Some think there are no dragons; nay, 'tis said
There was no George; pray God there was a maid.
                    Anonymous lines on England's patron saint

Generalities from Both Sides

Lang beards heartless, painted hoods witless, gay coats graceless, mak' England thriftless.

> Early Scottish view of the English

A fiery ettercap,   [spider]
A fractious chiel,
As het as ginger,   [hot]
And as stieve as steel.

> English characterisation of the medieval Scot

For every nation regards another nation as barbarous when their two natures and complexions are contrary to theirs, and there are not two nations under the firmament that are more contrary and different to each other than Englishmen and

Scotsmen, howbeit they be within one island, and of one language. For Englishmen are subtle and Scotsmen facile, Englishmen are ambitious in prosperity and Scotsmen are humane in prosperity, Englishmen are humble when they are subdued by force and violence, and Scotsmen are furious when they are violently subdued. Englishmen are cruel when they get victory, and Scotsmen are merciful when they get victory. And to conclude, it is impossible that Scotsmen and Englishmen can remain in concord under one government because their natures and conditions are as different as is the nature of sheep and wolves.

The Complaynt of Scotland (1549)

I wondered not, when I was told
The venal Scot his country sold;
I rather very much admire
How he could ever find a buyer.

Anonymous English verse, c. 1780

If the eating of Turds would come into fashion,
One Scotchman might then feed the whole English Nation.

Eighteenth-century English quip

A greedy, dark, degenerate place of Sin
For th' Universe to shoot her rubbish in …
Pimps, Bullies, Traitors, Robbers, 'tis all one,
Scotland, like wide-jaw'd Hell, refuses none.

Anonymous, from
A Trip Lately to Scotland (1705)

The Scots are like dung – no good unless spread.

> Old saying quoted by Alastair Reid
> in the *New Yorker* (1964)

Why do we always get Julians and Timothys? Let's get some Wullies in charge.

> Anonymous protest against the appointment
> of an Englishman as director of the National
> Galleries, quoted in A. Cran and J. Robertson,
> *Dictionary of Scottish Quotations* (1996)

What is a Scot but an uninspired Irishman?

> Anonymous remark noted in Forsyth Hardy,
> *John Grierson's Scotland* (1979)

Except in Scotland.

> Phrase found throughout *British Tastes:
> Likes and Dislikes of the Regional Consumer*
> by D. Elliston Allen (1968)

The Scotch are not that civil and polite people they are represented to be; if they are fawning, it is only to bite you – they are excellent Flatterers.

> Peter Barber, *Journey in Scotland*, 1795

The Scots are an Awful Retribution. They are to the English what the English are to the Continent. They just have a natural consciousness of their own superiority. And because they take it so for granted, the English have an uneasy sneaking sort of feeling that there may be something in it.

> Theodora Benson and
> Betty Askwith, *Foreigners* (1936)

Up amid the swells of London,
Mid the pomp of purple sinners,
Where many a kilted thane was undone,
With dice, debauchery, and dinners.
John Stuart Blackie (1809–1895)

The devellysche dysposicion of a Scottis man, not to love nor favour an Englis man … Trust yow no Skott.
Andrew Boorde, English spy, letter to
Thomas Cromwell from Scotland, 1536

The great Englishman is always a lunatic with a strongly practical side.
James Bridie,
A Small Stir

Yes, sir, the Englishman is amiable. He is the mildest mannered man ever to have scuttled ship or cut a throat.
James Bridie,
A Small Stir

The darling object of the English was to subjugate the Scotch; and if anything could increase the disgrace of so base an enterprise, it would be that, having undertaken it, they ignominiously failed.
Henry Thomas Buckle, *History of*
Civilization in England, Vol. III (1857)

… for the most part the worst instructed, and the least knowing of their rank, I ever went amongst.
Gilbert Burnet (1643–1715), *History of His*
Own Times, on the English aristocracy

Thirty millions, mostly fools.

> Thomas Carlyle (1795–1881), when
> asked what the population of England was

They're Citizens o' th' World; they're all in all, Scotland's a Nation epidemicall.

> John Cleveland (1613–58),
> *The Rebell Scot*

First Younger Sister to the Frozen Zone,
Battered by Parent Nature's constant Frown,
Adept to Hardships, and cut out for Toil;
The best worst Climate and the worst best Soil.

> Daniel Defoe (1660–1731), *Caledonia*

The Englishman remains everlastingly adolescent.

> Norman Douglas (1868–1952), *Old Calabria*

subsidy junkies

> The London *Evening Standard*, 1987,
> quoted in Maurice Smith, *Paper Lions: the
> Scottish Press and National Identity* (1994)

… the foul hordes of Scots and Picts like dark throngs of worms … a set of bloody freebooters, with more hair on their thievish faces than clothes to cover their nakedness.

> Gildas (c. 493–570), *De Excidio et Conquestu
> Britanniae*, on the Picts, from Latin

An Englishman is a man who lives on an island in the North Sea governed by Scotsmen.

> Philip Guedalla, *Supers and Supermen* (1920)

I have never hated the English, though I have frequently pitied them. A people who have so frequently been conquered is to be pitied, but that is another matter. They have this saving grace, however, when they come among us. They train easily and civilise very quickly, most of them, anyway. But gang warily when you get under an Englishman's skin. Before you get very deep you reach a thick layer of woad.

> Ian Hamilton, *The Taking of the
> Stone of Destiny* (new edn, 1991)

… if one will only read the anecdotes of village 'loonies' with which Scots literature abounds … he will find that the average Scots idiot was a creature of considerably more humour than the average Englishman.

> J. A. Hammerton, *J. M. Barrie
> and His Books* (1900)

... there is perhaps a natural hardness and want of sensibility about the Scotch, which renders them (rules and the consideration of consequences apart) not very nice or scrupulous in their proceedings ... Their impudence is extreme, their malice is cold-blooded, covert, crawling, deliberate, without the frailty or excuse of passion ... of all blackguards ... a Scotch blackguard is the worst.

> William Hazlitt (1778–1830),
> *On the Scotch Character*

Scotland is of all other countries in the world, perhaps the one in which the question 'What is the use of that?' is most often asked.

> William Hazlitt

I feel England and Scotland will only ever be happy together if they are politically apart.

> Simon Heffer, *Daily Telegraph*,
> 14 November 2007

The Barbarians who inhabit the banks of the Thames.

> David Hume (1711–1776),
> letter to Hugh Blair, April 1764

I am delighted to see the daily and hourly progress of Madness and Folly and Wicked-ness in England. The Consummation of these Qualities are the true Ingredients for making a fine Narrative in History, especially if followed by some signal and ruinous Convulsion, – as I hope will soon be the Case with that pernicious People.

> David Hume,
> *Letters*, 1769

Sir, it is not so much to be lamented that Old England is lost, as that the Scotch have found it.

> Samuel Johnson (1709–1784),
> to James Boswell, 15 May 1776

In all my travels I never met with any one Scotchman but what was a man of sense. I believe everybody of that country that has any, leaves it as fast as they can.

> Dr Francis Lockier (c.1669–1740)

Since the Union with England, Scotland's has been simply the role of caterpillar-grub stung into immobility by devouring wasp.

> Hugh MacDiarmid,
> *Lucky Poet* (1943)

To an Englishman something is what it is called: to a Scotsman, something is what it is.

> Sir Compton Mackenzie (1883–1972)

A sick, skint nation. The sooner we take them off the payroll, the better.

> Kelvin Mackenzie, one-time
> editor of *The Sun*, on the Scots

Despite everything I may say about the arrogance, tactlessness and insensitivity of the English … I can't help liking them.

> James Bridie and Moray McLaren,
> *A Small Stir* (1949)

Boswell was praising the English highly, and saying they were a fine, open people. 'Oh –,' said Macpherson, 'an open people! their mouths, indeed, are open to gluttony to fill their belly, but I know of no other openness they have.'

James Macpherson (1734–1796),
quoted in Charles Rogers, *Boswelliana* (1874)

At Babel names from pride and discord flowed;
And ever since men with a female spite
First call each other names, and then they fight.
Scotland and England! Cause of just uproar,
Do man and wife signify rogue and whore?

Andrew Marvell (1621–78),
The Loyal Scot

A Scotsman … does not thank you if you call him an Englishman

George Orwell (1903–50),
The Lion and the Unicorn

Scotland costs us, nags us, and grinds on. She may be surprised at how easily and comfortably we let her go.

Edward Pearce,
Guardian, January 1992

What makes Scotland Scotland is fast disappearing.

Sir Walter Scott
(1771–1832)

The English! My God, they ruffle my feathers. They strut this earth like medieval popes. They behave as if God has granted them divine right to be smug. We've fought their wars for them, colonized the world for them, propped up their rotten empire, and cleaned up the middens they've left behind from

Belfast to Borneo. And in Whitehall and Westminister and all along their corridors of power they treat us as if we were savages, still painted in woad. A subject race of congenital idiots, a nation of Harry Lauders with curly sticks and wee daft dugs, and stags at bay, and flying haggises and tartan dollies and Annie Lauries and hoots mon Jock McKay ye'll be a' richt the nicht if ye can hough-magandie backwards.

W. Gordon Smith, *Mr Jock* (1987)

I think, for my part, one half the nation is mad – and I find the other not very sound.

Tobias Smollett (1721–1771),
The Adventures of Launcelot Greaves

Scotland seems, indeed, the natural foyer of rebellion, as Egypt is of the plague.

John Wilkes (1727–97), to the
House of Commons

It is of Inglis natioune
The common kind conditioune
Of Trewis the wertu to forget,   [truth] [virtue]
And rekles of gud Faith to be.

Andrew of Wintoun (c.1350–c1424),
Orygynalle Cronykil of Scotland

Out of the Mouths of Babes

There was, and still is, a big difference in the development of national self-awareness of Scottish and English children. As young English children learn the account of their country's history, they discover the wives of Henry VIII, Armada, Empire, the Industrial Revolution. As presented, it is an open, expansive, positive story. Apart from the Union of the Crowns, and the Union of the Parliaments, Scotland plays little part in it compared with France, Spain and Holland. When young Scots come to discover the facts of their country's history, the huge part played by England makes a deep impression, and not a favourable one. Two writers have articulated this moment of realisation very clearly, on behalf of many others. The first is Robert Burns, in an autobiographical letter:

Robert Burns

'The story of Wallace poured a Scottish prejudice in my veins which will boil along there till the floodgates of life shut in eternal rest.'

The second is Hugh Miller, whose sense of national belonging was also awakened by Blind Harry's *Wallace*:

> I first became thoroughly a Scot in my tenth year; and the consciousness of country has remained tolerably strong within me ever since ... I was intoxicated with

the fiery narrative of the blind minstrel, with his fierce breathings of hot, intolerant patriotism, and his stories of astonishing prowess; and, glorying in being a Scot, and the country-man of Wallace and the Graham, I longed for a war with the Southron, that the wrongs and sufferings of these noble heroes might yet be avenged.

Not only boys felt such passion: this is from the childhood reminiscences of the brilliant Scottish mathematician whose name is commemorated in Somerville College, Oxford:

In our play-hours we amused ourselves with playing at ball, marbles, and especially at 'Scotch and English', a game which represented a raid on the debatable land, or Border between Scotland and England, in which each party tried to rob the other of their playthings. The little ones were always compelled to be English, for the bigger girls thought it was too degrading.

Mary Somerville (1780–1872),
Personal Recollections from Early Life

The twentieth-century Scottish children's writer Lavinia Derwent, who grew up very near the Border, recalled a similar attitude from her own childhood: 'Only a stone's throw away lay a strange foreign country – England! I was told the natives were an unfriendly lot. Indeed they were our bitterest enemies, waiting for an opportunity to slink across the Border, steal our cattle and sheep, and burn down our abbeys ...' When the young Lavinia went to school, as a 'Mixed Infant', she met an English girl: 'my first foreigner ... I fought the battle bravely, but lost. The result: my first black eye, which I richly deserved. I was quite proud of it for a time, and then a strange thing happened. We became firm friends.'

This strong sense of nationality could make life difficult for English children who were brought to Scotland. The nineteenth-century writer George Borrow recalled his first Edinburgh schooldays in *Lavengro*:

'Scotland is a better country than England,' said an ugly, blear-eyed boy, about a head and shoulders taller than myself, the leader of a gang of varlets who surrounded me in the play-ground, on the first day, as soon as the morning lesson was over. 'Scotland is a far better country than England, in every respect.'

'Is it?' said I. 'Then you ought to be very thankful for not having been born in England.'

'That's just what I am, ye loon; and every morning, when I say my prayers, I thank God for not being an Englishman. The Scotch are a much better and braver people than the English.'

'It may be so,' said I, 'for what I know – indeed, till I came here, I never heard a word either about the Scotch or their country.'

'Are ye making fun of us, ye English puppy?' said the blear-eyed lad; 'take that!' and I was presently

beaten black and blue. And thus did I first become aware of the difference of races and their antipathy to each other.

'Bow to the storm, and it shall pass over you.' I held my peace, and silently submitted to the superiority of the Scotch, in numbers. This was enough; from an object of persecution I soon became one of patronage, especially among the champions of the class.

'The English,' said the blear-eyed lad, 'though a wee bit behind the Scotch in strength and fortitude, are nae to be sneezed at, being far ahead of the Irish, to say nothing of the French, a pack of scoundrels. And with regard to the English country, it is na Scotland, it is true, but it has its gude properties; and, though there is ne'er a haggis in a' the land, there's an unco deal o' gowd and siller. I respect England, for I have an auntie married there.'

Trevor Royle experienced the conflicting pressures on an English boy growing up in Scotland during the 1950s:

I had learned enough to get by and to survive and, more importantly from a child's point of view, to merge into the background. I remained on the outside … I could never (and this was a test) feel the intense dismay and dislike of the English that my friends felt. And why should I, being one myself? … When we were in Scotland we were unmistakably English, but in the South the mantle of the Scot was thrust upon us. Despite our surnames we were 'Scotties' or 'Jocks' and people smiled at the way we rolled our 'r's (how I tired of that sly joke). After a week or two we became more Scottish than the Scots and in the absence of critical countrymen boasted about our adopted country's superiority.

An Observer of the Scots: Sydney Smith

Sydney Smith, the celebrated English clergyman and wit, lived for five years in Edinburgh between 1798 and 1803. He was the prime founder of the *Edinburgh Review*, though his colleagues refused to accept his motto for the journal, 'We cultivate literature on a little oatmeal', and kept up the connection long after his return to England. Some of his comments on the Scots are well-known. The most famous, that 'It requires a surgical operation to get a joke well into a Scotch understanding' is a tease – Smith happily played up to Scottish susceptibilities. Any suggestion that they lacked a sense of humour was bound to make them rise. But some of his remarks are more penetrating, like: 'A Scotchman always says what is undermost.' He joins a long train of his fellow-countrymen in remarking on the smells and related hazards of Edinburgh, despite its beauties:

> Taste guides my eye, where e'er new beauties spread,
> While prudence whispers 'look before you tread'.

Smith also probed other sensitive areas:

> Their temper stands anything but an attack on their climate. They would have you even believe that they can ripen fruit; and, to be candid, I must own in remarkably warm summers I have tasted peaches that made

most excellent pickles; and it is upon record that at the
siege of Perth, on one occasion, their ammunition
failing, their nectarines made admirable cannon balls.

Smith liked to picture the Scots as idealists, obsessed by
abstract ideas, too analytical in their approach to everything.
The English, by contrast, he saw as pragmatists, synthesizers,
looking for links, not breaks. In a letter to his friend John Allen
(one of the many Scottish doctors in London), he wrote:

If you were sailing from Alicant to Aleppo in a storm,
and, after the sailors had held up the image of a saint
and prayed to it, the storm were to abate, you would
be more sorry for the encouragement of superstition
than rejoiced at the preservation of your life; and so
would every other man born and bred in Edinburgh.
My views of the matter would be much shorter and
coarser: I should be so glad to find myself alive, that I
should not care a farthing if the storm had generated a
thousand new, and revived as many old saints.

Sydney Smith
observing Scotland

Sensing a certain intellectual arrogance in the rigours of Scottish thought, Smith characterised it in his digest of the views of the universe held by his friend Francis Jeffrey, editor of the *Edinburgh Review*: 'Damn the solar system! – bad lights – planets too distant – pestered with comets – feeble contrivance; could make a better one with great ease.' He urged Jeffrey to be less analytical: 'Because others build slightly and eagerly, you employ yourself in kicking down their houses, and contract a sort of aversion for the more honourable, useful and difficult task of building well yourself.'

A Would-be Scourge of
Scotland – *The Unspeakable Scot*

In *The Rise and Fall of the Man of Letters* (1969), John Gross makes a passing reference to 'Lord Alfred Douglas and his obnoxious henchman, T.W.H. Crosland.' Douglas – Oscar Wilde's 'Bosie' – was an Anglo-Scot. Crosland, a literary hack with pretensions to poetry, was the author of a book which once enjoyed some notoriety, *The Unspeakable Scot*, published in 1902. The publisher intended it as the first of a series which would satirise or lampoon various nationalities, but this and

T.W.H. Crosland

Crosland's *Taffy* were the only ones to appear. 'This book is for Englishmen', it announces. Sadly, it is rather boring, with little in it to arouse Scottish fire. Its targets are mostly forgotten figures and long-outdated literary cliques and styles, and the techniques and phraseology of anti-semitism, which he held to more sincerely than anti-Scotism, frequently show through: 'Your proper child of Caledonia believes in his rickety bones that he is the salt of the earth. Prompted by a glozing pride, not to say by a black and consuming avarice, he has proclaimed his saltiness from the housetops in and out of season, unblushingly, assiduously, and with results which have no doubt been most satisfactory from his own point of view.' It is a poor last gasp of the robust tradition maintained by Charles Churchill in the eighteenth century. The endpaper of *The Unspeakable Scot* promises *The Egregious Englishman*, by one Angus MacNiell, but it never appeared.

An Observer of the English: A.G. MacDonell

England, Their England, by A.G. Macdonell, first published in 1933, is one of the best-known portrayals of the English by a Scot. It is written as fiction, describing the discovery of England by a young and naïve Scot who plans to write a book on 'The English Character'. A kindly book, written with a light touch, and set among the literary and upper classes, it presents a limited picture, though it is striking how little – in many ways – has changed in the ensuing decades. The hero, Donald Cameron, searching for 'typical Englishmen', finds there is no such thing. Instead he encounters a nation of individuals, linked by a variety of different codes and by

A.G. Macdonell
observing England

whom life seems to be regarded as a game played by arcane and unwritten rules. To the earnest-minded Donald, their flippancy is often mystifying, but their seriousness is equally baffling. In one episode, he has just watched a fox-hunt, in which the fox, run to earth, was dug out and killed: 'because, after all, the country-side must be saved from vermin even if ladies and gentlemen have to chase them on horseback for an hour and a half, and furthermore it would be an act of callous cruelty to dumb animals, which no Englishman could be guilty of, to deprive the sixty dogs of the midday meal which they had so bravely earned.' The satire, of a gentle sort, is mostly directed against the interconnecting worlds of Literature and Society, with an emphasis on the country-house weekend. The kind of Englishman the author most clearly respects is the hard-working practical engineer Mr Rhodes, and the old fellows who sit in rustic pubs and utter such phrases as: 'Well, has anyone got their antirrhinums in yet?' In the penultimate scene Donald is trapped on the roof of the burning Hotel Joséphine with a collection of people he has come to know, and to regard as rather flashy and febrile:

'Ladies and gentlemen,' said the Major-General, rising to his feet and rapping on the table, 'I am the senior officer present. You will kindly regard me as Officer Commanding Joséphine Roof Garden.'

Murmurs of 'Hear, hear,' 'Agreed', and some slight applause greeted this announcement.

Once they ascertain there is no way down, they settle down to wait and see which will happen first, a fiery death or arrival of the fire brigade. One of the party is a film actress:

'It's a bit hard to be asked to face one's Maker without a single flashlight man,' she said.

'Never mind,' said Mr Harcourt, looking over the parapet down into Park Lane, 'you are going to play to capacity in your farewell performance. The house is filling up beautifully.'

'Positively the last appearance,' said Mr Huggins.

'Miss d'Avenant literally finished in a blaze,' said Mr Harcourt.

– to which darkly humorous remarks the actress replies, 'Sweet pets.'

The ladder appears in the nick of time, and – ladies first – they descend in disciplined order.

The implicit comment is that, in emergency, the English become cohesive and effective without losing their coolness or humour. Although the novel points out some of the inconsistencies of the English way of life and state of mind, what comes most strongly from it is the author's sense of admiration at a country which – so unlike Scotland – feels no need to compare itself with anywhere else. All its characters share a self-sufficient serenity in their Englishness. Macdonell himself, incidentally, was sent to Winchester College and later lived in England.

In the first chapter, a Welshman is chatting to Donald: 'We had an English subaltern once in our battery who used to run and extinguish fires in ammunition dumps … He said that shells cost five pounds each and it was everyone's duty to save government money.'

'Where is he buried?' asked Cameron.

Aspects of Difference: Dress

'They're always getting themselves up in fancy dress. They adore fancy-dress. Look at their Beefeaters, and their Chelsea Pensioners, and their barristers' wigs, and their peers' robes, and the Beadle of the Bank of England, and the Lord Mayor's Show ... Show an Englishman a fancy-dress, and he puts it on.' So wrote A.G. Macdonell in *England, Their England*, doubtless tongue-in-cheek, being himself a one-time kilted soldier in the 51st Highland Division.

But in the matter of costume, the humour traffic has always been largely one-way, from south to north. There may be some quite bizarre forms of dress in England, like that of Morris dancers with their knotted hankies, bells and garlands, but Morris dancing is the pursuit of a very small number, and they are certainly not wearing the national dress. Scotland by contrast has one of the most conspicuous 'national' costumes, for males, in the world. This is not the place to go into the origins of Highland dress, apart from one thing. Some English commentators have rejoiced in pointing out that the kilt, in its present form, was devised by an Englishman, Thomas Rawlinson, manager of the iron-works in Glen Garry, from 1727 to 1734, as an alternative to the belted plaid which was too cumbersome a garment for his Highland workers. There is great pleasure to be had in the thought that this flaunted sign of Scottishness is owed to an Englishman. It is around this time that the Scots word 'kilt' first appears, perhaps with the sense of 'gathered up': a woman kilted her long skirts if she had to walk through mud or water; the Gaelic word, rendered in English as 'philabeg', has no relation to it. But though Rawlinson, like many a Scottish-based Englishman to follow, is said to have taken up wearing the kilt himself, there is no real evidence that he pioneered the pleated kilt design, which is more likely to have been devised by a travelling tailor. His fellow countryman Edmund Burt makes numerous references to the 'quelt' and its brevity, in his own description of Highlanders, and Burt left the Highlands the year before Rawlinson arrived. Long before that, Highlanders wearing the long plaid, the *feille mòr* or 'great kilt', had attracted the notice of the wider world. 'Redshanks' was the usual name, in reference to their bare legs, given to them by the English in Ireland. It is doubtful if many kilted Scots reached England until the arrival of Prince Charles Edward Stuart's army in 1745. After that episode, the kilt was firmly ingrained into English consciousness as an attribute of the Scots.

William Murray, fourth son of the Earl of Stormont, born in 1705 in the then somewhat ramshackle Scone Castle,

became the Lord Chief Justice of England, as Lord Mansfield. He was sent to Westminster School at the age of fourteen, but prior to that had gone to the grammar school of Perth. London's Grub Street pamphleteers liked to mock at Mansfield's early years as a kilted Scottish schoolboy: 'Learning was very cheap in his country, and it is very common to see a boy of quality lug along his books to school, and a scrap of oatmeal for his dinner, with a pair of brogues on his feet, posteriors exposed, and nothing on his legs.'

In the days when men wore knee-breeches, and fastened them at the knee with a buckle, someone developed a special patent buckle, and sued another man who had copied it. In the London court, counsel for the prosecution was the Scot Thomas Erskine, later to be lord chancellor. He held up the patent buckle to the jury, expatiating on its merits as a fastener. 'How would my ancestors have admired this specimen of dexterity,' he exclaimed. The opposing counsel, an Englishman, had an answer ready: 'Gentlemen,' he said to the jury, 'you have heard a good deal today of my learned friend's ancestors and their probable astonishment at his knee-buckles. But gentlemen, I can assure you, their astonishment would have been quite as great at his breeches.'

When Sydney Smith wrote about a political mob: 'did not the Scotch philosophers tear off the clothes of the Tories in Mintoshire?' he could not forbear from adding, '… or at least such clothes as the custom of the country admit of being worn?'

Ironically, of course, it is only since the visit of King George IV to Edinburgh in 1832 that the kilt has become 'national' – before that it was regarded by Lowland Scots as a primitive and far from respectable costume. Lord Macaulay, commenting on the king 'disguising himself in what, before the Union, was considered by nine Scotchmen out of ten as the dress of a thief' remarked: 'As long as the Gaelic dress was worn, the

Saxons had pronounced it hideous, ridiculous, nay, grossly indecent. Soon after it had been prohibited, they discovered it was the most graceful drapery in Europe.'

Nowadays kilt jokes remain popular outside and even inside Scotland, when not insulting:

> When the good Lord made the Jocks, he did not design
> them to go upstairs in tramcars.
> W. Gordon Smith

> Queen Victoria, to kilted Scot: Is anything worn under
>   the kilt?
> Kilted Scot: No, ma'am, it's all in perfect working order.
>   (I believe this joke originated with the
>   colonial-born Irish-Englishman Spike Milligan.)

A nineteenth-century *Punch* joke was made in a two-stage drawing.

Scene One – Cockney Tourist, to Scotsman in High-land dress, who is leaning against the wall of a bridge:

'Hey, Scotty, show us the Highland fling!'

Scene Two – The Scotsman tosses the Cockney Tourist over the bridge and into the river.

Question: What does a Scotsman wear under his kilt?
Answer: Socks and shoes.

But there are others of a cruder sort, obsessed with gender and sex, and not safe to tell north of the Border:

Why do Scotsmen wear kilts?
So that the sheep won't hear zips being undone.

Aspects of Difference:
Food and Drink

A report published in November 2011 asserted that if the Scots (and the Welsh and the Northern Irish) adopted a diet similar to that of the English, and ate more vegetables, salad, etc., there would be several thousand fewer deaths each year. Presumably it meant premature or unnecessary deaths – after all, death may be deferred but not avoided – but it pinpoints a cultural-historical difference. After a long history of bland if nutritious fare in which oatmeal, and more lately the potato, played a large part, the Scots are still gorging on sweet and fatty foods.

Neither the English nor the Scots stand high in the list of culinary nations. Both have been blasted for their indifference to good cooking and the amenities of the table, and neither country was considered to have anything to teach others about cookery. The Frenchman Faujas de St-Fond in the eighteenth century remarked that 'the English and Scotch attach no importance to the fine perfume and flavour of good coffee for it seems to be all one to them what kind they drink, provided they have four or five cupfuls'. The Neapolitan ambassador, Carraciolo, famously remarked that the English had thirty kinds of religion, but only one sauce. For that reason, perhaps, there is not a great deal of banter exchanged on food topics. The English used to enjoy the story about the hotel guest who came downstairs on his first morning in Scotland and saw porridge for the first time. He complained to the manager that someone had been sick on his plate. With their range of ethnic dishes that included haggis, the Scots provided another distinctive aspect for the English to tease. The French could, and did, mock the cooking of England; the Scots were not in a position to do this. Nevertheless, whatever the culinary and hygienic standards the English used to face at home, most of them found Scotland worse: 'I observed no Art of Cookery, or furniture of Household stuff, but rather rude neglect of both,' wrote the English visitor Fynes Morison in 1598.

> 'There is great store of fowl,' observed Sir Anthony Weldon, going on to commit a foul pun: 'as foul houses, foul sheets, foul linen, foul dishes and pots … They have good store of fish too, and good for those that can eat it raw; but if it come once into their hands, it is worse than if it were three days old: for their butter and cheese, I will not meddle withal at this time, nor no man else at any time that loves his life.'

'Their pewter pots, wherein they bring wine and water, are furred within, that it would loathe you to touch anything that comes out of them', shuddered Sir William Brereton in 1636.

'To come into their kitchen, and see them dress their meat, and to behold the sink (which is more offensive than any jakes) will be a sufficient supper, and will take off the edge of your stomach.'

Thomas Kirke echoed his words forty-three years later:

To put one's head into their kitchen doors is little less than destructive; you enter Hell alive, where the black furies are busy in mangling dead carcases and the fire and brimstone, or rather stew and stink, is ready to suffocate you ...

When Edmund Burt visited Edinburgh in 1725, he had already encountered the Scots' notion of hygiene at Kelso, but still:

the cook was too filthy an object to be described; only another English gentleman whispered me and said, he believed, if the fellow was to be thrown against the wall, he would stick to it.

Very occasionally, a Scot has felt sufficient confidence to denigrate English cooking: 'Even a boiled egg tastes of mutton fat in England', noted Norman Douglas in *Old Calabria*.

Of haggis, now so closely associated with Scotland, it must be said that it is first found mentioned in England, in the *Liber Cocorum*, or Book of Cooks, one of the earliest cookbooks. That was in 1402; and there is evidence from other writings, culinary and otherwise, that the haggis remained a popular dish there for several centuries. One of the comic characters in Ben Jonson's seventeenth-century play *Bartholomew Fair* is 'Haggis – a watchman'. He is no Scottish immigrant but a pure Cockney. It seems likely that haggis declined in England, its demise spreading northwards. But in Scotland, it kept its popularity. In this respect, as with bagpipe music, Scotland preserved a worthy old European custom which the fashions of richer and trendier countries disdained.

A Scotsman died, and having led a good and blameless life, duly presented himself at the entrance gate of Heaven.
    'What is your name?' asked St Peter.
    'Archibald MacNab.'
    'Are you Scottish by any chance?'
    'Indeed I am.'
    'Then you can't come in. We're not making haggis for one.'

Of Scots ale, Richard Franck remarked in 1656, 'so thick and roapy it was, you might eat it with spoons'. The Scots were greater drinkers than the English, and frequently had better wine: no visitors complained about the quality of their claret. Even Scots admitted the English were more temperate. When James Hogg, author of *Confessions of a Justified Sinner*, went to London in 1832, he wrote to his wife: 'The people here are all sober there being no deep drinking here as in Scotland … I have not seen one drunk person neither poor not rich.'

Whatever the origins of whisky (the Irish have made claims) it is of interest in any Scottish–English comparison that the Scots should have created or developed a fiery spirit as the national alcoholic drink, while the English, with other Teutonic nations, drank beer. A difference in temperament might be assumed, but it is more probably an accident of geography that water, peat and barley happened to coincide, with fortunate results for the Scottish economy, if not for the

Scots' livers. They still drink more whisky per head of the population than any other nation. But the industry, and the 'whisky reserves', are also caught up in the argument about whether a Scottish state could keep its people in the style to which they have become accustomed.

A Scottish climber was high up in the Alps with a friend from England when they both were caught in a snow slide. Luckily it was a small one, and, though bruised and battered, they were able to cling to some rocks and wait for a rescue party to arrive. The first sign of rescue was a huge St Bernard dog that loomed up out of the snow, the traditional barrel of brandy tucked under its chin.

'Ah, look, Man's best friend,' said the Englishman.

'Yes,' said the Scotsman enthusiastically, 'and look at the size of the dog that's carrying it.'

Aspects of Difference: Humour

Do the Scots and the English laugh at the same things? Generally speaking, yes. Humour is a universal human attribute and most people laugh at the same sort of things. Strangely, the people who look for resemblances between the English and the Scots tend to overlook the fact that the humour of both is almost identical. They laugh at the same things, express their sense of the comic in similar ways, and share a taste for word-based jokes and dark, sometimes macabre comedy.

The favourite English joke of the English writer Hilaire Belloc was said to be this: A man gets into a railway compartment, which already has a single occupant. The occupant immediately begins to tell the new arrival all his dreadful troubles, and ends by asking, 'What would you do in my position?'

'I believe I should cut my throat,' is the answer.

'That's just what I have done,' replies the sad one, raising his chin to show a ghastly slash, and expires.

Here is a specimen of Glaswegian humour:

First man: Has yer mither got a sewing machine?
Second man: Whit if she has?
First man: Well, see if she can stitch *that*.
(the swish of an opened razor is heard)

Second man: Ha, ha, ye missed.
First man: Try shakin' yer heid.

Of these two examples of cut-throat humour, the Scottish one is more succinct, and leaves more to the imagination. It does a more effective job, and so is a better joke, but an English reader would appreciate it just as much as a Scottish one. Scottish humour has suffered from being typecast as 'pawky' – wry, sly humour. Undoubtedly it is a specialism, but the range is much wider, though perhaps not so wide as English humour, which is the most universal in the world, from the crude to the cerebral. Enough examples are quoted elsewhere in this book to demonstrate that in terms ranging from humorous comment to downright insult, the two sides are evenly matched. But as Allan Massie notes in *The Thistle and the Rose*, the English also have an ability to laugh at themselves, something the Scots have never been good at. In 1611 King James VI spent the very large sum of £600 to procure the execution in Poland of one Stercovius, a Pole who had visited Scotland, and, having been roughly treated or otherwise insulted by the natives, had published a satire upon the Scots. James tried without success to get the Scottish burghs to repay the cost of the exercise.

Aspects of Difference: Music

In recent times, musicians have moved smoothly between England and Scotland. Sir Peter Maxwell Davies famously made Orkney his home. James Macmillan is appreciated south of the Border. But English attention to Scottish music has always focused on the bagpipe. Once upon a time it was the most common musical instrument in Europe. Its materials were readily available and it was cheap to make. Providing the player with an extra lung, it was able to produce sustained sound, and its range could encompass the wedding dance, the funeral lament and the battle charge. But by the end of the Middle Ages, the bagpipe had become obsolete almost everywhere in western Europe except Scotland. The Scots not only kept it but developed a new form of music for it, the pibroch.

English rudeness about the bagpipes is not new:

> Musick they have, but not the harmony of the sphears, but loud terrene noises, like the bellowing of beasts; the loud bagpipe is their chief delight.
>
> Thomas Kirke,
> *A Modern Account of Scotland* (1679)

The pipes, like all unusual and distinctive musical instruments, suffer from the rash of one-dimensional internet-type jokes.

What's the difference between a bagpipe and an onion?
No-one cries when you chop up a bagpipe.

How do you get two pipers to play in unison?
Shoot one of them.

Definition of a gentleman: someone who knows how
to play the bagpipes – and doesn't.

Did you hear about the piper who left his pipes lying
on the back seat of his car? Someone broke the window
and left another set of pipes alongside them.

But the pipes have the last word. As W. Gordon Smith noted,
they are also: '… terror in the hearts of the enemy. The greatest
laxative in the world.'

'The English are a funny people,' remarked Hamish, on his return from a holiday south of the Border. 'I was in my hotel room one night, walking up and down, playing a few tunes on the pipes, and someone came hammering on the door and shouted "Make less noise!"

'What did you do?' asked his friend.

'I took my boots off,' said Hamish.

It has been said that the English actually secretly love the bagpipes, but this is only partially correct: what they love is the spectacle and the sense of experiencing something a little wilder than everyday existence usually offers. The Scots have not mocked at any musical tradition preserved by the English, though they may have searched to find one.

Aspects of Difference: The Sexes

In the old cross-Border relationship, women played a greater role on the Scottish side, where there was a tradition of the 'woman warrior' to draw on, like Lylliard in the 15th century:

> Fair maiden Lylliard lies under this stane
> Little was her stature but great was her fame
> Upon the English louns she laid many thumps,
> And when her legs were cuttit off she fought upon the
> stumps.

Inscription recorded from
'Lilliard's Stone', Midlothian

Yet the most influential woman in Scottish history was English – the 11th-century West Saxon princess Margaret, second wife of King Malcolm III – an energetic reformer who swept out much of the nation's old ways, and whose sons might be considered the first Anglo-Scots.

Men are quoted more often than women in this book, a reflection of the way in which men used to dominate public discourse. In that context, women could be targets. In the *Satire Against Scotland*, written in 1617, and generally ascribed to him, Sir Anthony Weldon remarks: 'Thair beastis be generallie small (women excepted), of which sort thair ar no greater in the world.' This is tame beside what he goes on to say: '… their flesh naturally abhors cleanliness; their body smells of sweat, and their splay feet never offend in socks. To be chained in marriage with one of them, were to be tied to a dead carcass, and cast into a stinking ditch; formosity and a dainty face are things they dream not of.'

In an *Answer* to this satire, a Scottish writer pretending to be one of Weldon's fellow countrymen says: 'This unclean beast found your wemen too honest for his purpose, and thairfoir voued to plague them thus with his pen.'

An anonymous English writer, a century later, remarked in *Scotland Characterized*: 'Their Women are, if possible, worse than the Men, and carry no Temptations ... Their Voice is like Thunder ... It is a very Common Thing for a Woman of Quality to say to her Footman, "Andrew, take a fast Gripe of my Arse, and help me over the Stile."

The traveller Thomas Pennant remarked, of Scottish women: 'The common women are in general most remarkably plain, and soon acquire an old look, and by being much exposed to the weather without hats, such a grin, and contraction of muscles as heightens greatly their natural hardness of features: I never saw so much plainness among the lower rank of females: but the *ne plus ultra* of hard features is not found until you arrive among the fishwives of Aberdeen.'

A Scottish ballad of 1634 claims that Scots lasses were impervious to English advances, preferring the 'Blew Cap' of the Scotsman:

> There lived a blithe lass in Faukeland towne,   [Falkland]
> And shee had some suitors, I wot not how many;   [know]
> But her resolution shee had set downe
> That shee'd have a Blew-Cap gif e'er she had any:
> An Englishman when our good king was there
> Came often unto her, and loved her deere:
> But still she replied, 'Sir, I pray let me be
> Gif ever I have a man, Blew-Cap for me.'
>
> > ['Our good king' refers to Charles I's
> > coronation visit to Scotland, in 1633.]

In any situation of national rivalry, however, as well as feminine beauty, virility will rise up as a contested area. The Scot, at least when attired in a swash-buckling kilt, probably has the advantage. An explanation is offered by the historian Linda Colley in her study of the forging of the British nation, *Britons*: 'The belief that Scottish Highlanders were unusually well endowed sexually was an old one in the Lowlands and England, reflecting the fact that – like blacks in the American south – they were seen as both threatening and primitive.'

In his satirical poem *The Prophecy of Famine*, Charles Churchill wrote of the Scots: 'Into our places, states and beds they creep' – a reference to Lord Bute's supposed affair with George III's mother. In, *Britons*, Linda Colley notes that in the 1760s, 'English insecurity in the face of this new Scottish leverage helps to explain the obsession in so much written and visual polemic at this time with Scottish sexual potency … as the princess was made to say in one splendidly filthy cartoon, her hand located firmly under Lord Bute's kilt: "A man of great parts is sure greatly to rise."'

… the average Englishman dislikes women. He dislikes them even more than the Lowland Scot dislikes them: and that's saying a good deal … It is the English who have invented all the ingenious devices for escaping from women's company.

James Bridie and Moray McLaren, *A Small Stir*

On his return from the House of Lords to the Tower, an old woman, not very well favoured, had pressed through the crowd and screamed in at the window of the coach, 'You'll get that nasty head of yours chopped off, you ugly old Scotch dog,' to which he answered, 'I believe I shall, you ugly old English bitch.'

John Hill Burton, *Life of Simon Lord Lovat* (1847), on the trial and execution of Lord Lovat in 1747

A Scottish soldier and an English soldier were walking in uniform along a canal bank, chatting together. They came to a place where a lusciously pretty girl was sitting, fishing.

'What are you fishing for?' asked the Jock.

'For men,' she replied, archly.

'How come you're sitting on your bait?' said the Jock.

The two soldiers walked on. For about half an hour the Englishman said nothing. Then finally he turned to his friend:

'Jock, that was an awfully funny thing you said to that girl. But how did you know she had worms?'

Aspects of Difference: Sport

In sports, Scots and English meet upon equal terms. There is no assumption that one side is specially good or specially bad. Much of each nation's most critical sporting humour is related to the shortcomings of the home side, and not relevant to this book.

An early international was played in 1599 when six Armstrongs from Liddesdale came across the border to Bewcastle to have a game of football with six English lads. Who won is not recorded. After the game they resorted to hard drinking. But there was treachery afoot. An Englishman, William Ridley, had set up an ambush to capture the Armstrongs, all of them wanted for various raids and crimes in England. His plan had been leaked, however, and his ambush was itself attacked by a heavy force. Ridley and two others were killed, thirty prisoners were taken, and 'many sore hurt, especially John Whytfeild whose bowells came out, but are sowed up agane'.

In recent times, there has been some indignation expressed in England when the Scots (their side having been already eliminated) have not rallied *en masse* in support of the English team, not yet eliminated, in competitions such as the football World Cup. There have even been A.B.E. (Anyone But England) tee-shirts. But the protesters fail to follow the Scottish logic. If the United Kingdom fields four national sides, there is no particular reason for supporters of any three to support the fourth if it happens to survive a little longer in the competition. Many Scots will do so, while others make other choices.

The Scottish attitude to English internationals was defined by Bill Shankly on his first game against England, in 1938: '... we were Scottish to the core. The wee lion on your dark blue shirt roared out "Get out and kill them." And your heart swelled twice the size.'

> I thought the greatest moment of my life was this year (1974) on the rain-soaked terraces of Hampden when that second goal went in and we'd beaten the white-shirted swines ... men, grown men were greetin' like ... this wee fellow next to me in a big tartan tammy, I threw him in the air. 'We've done it,' I was shouting, 'we've done it,' and there was no way they were going to get two goals back.
>
> And he said, as he was sort of coming down – well I exaggerate a trifle, but I did chuck him up – he said: 'I'm from Shepherd's Bush, mate.' I said, 'Well, what are you wearing that thing for?' And he said, 'It's only for protection, to get into the ground.'
>
> Gordon Williams

In 1961, it had been a different story. The only way the Scots could take any comfort from a 9–3 scoreline was when one fan remarked: 'Mind you, when was the last time we took three goals off England at Wembley?'

Although the English cultivate, or used to cultivate, the sense of sportsmanship, James Bridie observed that: 'You will notice that he commends his enemy with a sincere "Well played, Sir," only when he is obviously a beaten enemy.'

There is a joke which has been heard in Scotland: 'How does an Englishman get into the World Cup final? By being the referee.' But this is dangerous ground for Scots. The Scottish attitude at the start of any tournament in which the national side is involved has been described as 'Premature Jock elation'.

Jokes about national prowess are less common than jokes about players or supporters:

> The day before an International match, the English football side booked in to a big Glasgow hotel. They all came down to dinner together, the coach placing himself at the head of the table. He beckoned to the waiter and said:
>
> 'I'll have a twelve-ounce fillet steak, done medium rare.'
>
> 'And the vegetables, sir?' asked the waiter. The coach waved an expansive hand.
>
> 'Oh, they'll all have the same.'

> Scottish (or English) fan: What was the score?
> English (or Scottish) fan: Nil–nil.
> First fan: And at half-time?

In 1999 a Yorkshire brewery brought out a special ale called 'Goodbye, Jock' in anticipation of a Scotland–England game.

What do you need if you have the supporters of the English football side up to their necks in sand?

A few more tons of sand.

Graffito on a pillar of Kingston Bridge, Glasgow: English Go Home.

On the next pillar: Yes, with the Calcutta Cup.

When a leading English rugby player died, he found himself, to his surprise, at the gate of Heaven. St Peter was there, of course.

'We're letting you in here,' he said, 'despite everything, on account of your services to English rugby.'

'Okay,' said the player. 'Just one thing – are there any Scottish players in there?'

'Oh, no, certainly not,' said St Peter.

'That's all right, then,' said the player, and went in, and for the first few days was as happy as any resident of Heaven. But then, going along one day, he heard a roar behind a high wall. Reaching a gate, he went in, and found a rugby game in progress. The star was undoubtedly a tall player with flowing golden hair, golden boots – and wearing what was unmistakably a Scotland strip. The English player watched as the splendid figure scored try after try, converting each one flawlessly. In a rage he left the game amd stormed along to see St Peter.

'I thought you said there weren't any Scottish rugby players here,' he said, and described what he had seen.

'Oh,' said St Peter. 'That was just God. He likes to think He's Scottish.'

An English rugby fan met another in their Edinburgh hotel on the morning after England had beaten Scotland and won the Grand Slam at Murrayfield. The friend was sporting a massive black eye.

'Jeremy, old chap, what happened?'

'I was in a pub in the city centre last night, and we were having a perfectly normal discussion about the game, when suddenly this Scotsman leaned over and punched me for no apparent reason.'

Why do lots of English football teams have Scottish managers, and hardly any Scottish football teams have English managers? Because good managers can't afford to work in Scotland. And Scottish teams can't afford even bad English managers.

A top English Premier League side had a Scottish manager, and one of its top players had a glamorous pop-star wife. One afternoon, the manager announced he had to leave the training session early:

'Carry on, lads,' he said. 'Another two hours of ball-skills practice, then you can go home.'

As soon as he was gone, one of his mates said to the star:

'Why don't we go and have a game of golf instead? The boss will never know.'

'Good idea,' said the star.

So he jumped into his Ferrari and drove home to get his golf clubs. Hearing strange gasping noises from the bedroom, he looked in, and there was the manager vigorously making love to his wife. Quietly he tiptoed away.

On the next training session, the manager again said he had to leave early. His friend once again proposed a game of golf, but this time the ace player shook his head.

'Definitely not,' he said. 'You've no idea how near I got to being caught by the boss last time.'

Three small boys playing in a London street were hit by a garbage truck and killed instantly. Transported to heaven, they were met by St Peter, wringing his hands.

'It's all a dreadful mistake,' he said. 'We got the wrong street. I'm sorry. We're sending you straight back, and to make amends, each of you in twenty years' time will be at the top of his chosen profession. Just state your ambition as you jump off the edge of the cloud.'

The first to jump cried out: 'Lawyer!' Twenty years later he was appointed as a High Court judge.

The second called: 'Doctor!' Twenty years later, he was a highly-paid brain surgeon.

The third, as he stepped off, stumbled and almost tripped. 'Clumsy fool,' he muttered.

Twenty years later, he was named as captain of the England football side.

On the other hand, an English football expert was once asked what he thought of Scottish football.

'What a good idea,' he said. 'Why don't they give it a try?'

And, allegedly from BBC television: 'More on football later. But first, the Scottish Premier League results.'

Literary Encounters

When Robert Henryson's *Animal Fables* were first published in England, in 1577, as *The Fabulous Tales of Esope the Phrygian*, they were advertised as translated: 'Compiled moste eloquently in Scottisch Metre ... and now lately Englished'. Their translator, Richard Smith, notes the neglect of Scottish literature in England, and puts it down to political reasons, which he seems to share:

> But whether most men have that nation in derision for their hollowe hearts and ungratefull mindes to this country alwayes had (a people verie subject to that

infection) or thinking scorne of the Authour or first inventor let it passe.

– he doesn't care much, anyway. In the Prologue, written by himself, Smith makes Aesop-Henryson say of the English:

> They do not care for Scottish bookes,
> They list not looke that way:
> But if they would but cast their lookes
> Some time when they do play,
> Somewhat to see perhaps they might
> That then would like them wel,
> To teach then treade thair way aright
> To blisse, from paines of hel.

The English poet John Skelton attacked a Scot, Sir George Dundas, who had written a Latin poem reminding the world that Englishmen had tails. Part of his diatribe reads:

> Skelton laureat
> After this rate
> Defendeth with his pen
> All Englysh men
> Agayn Dundas
> That Scottishe asse
>
> Dundas, dronken and drowsy
> Skabed, scurvy and lowsy,
> Of unhappy generacion
> And most ungracious nacion.

By the seventeenth century the work of literary Scots no longer needed translation. When the Scottish lawyer and writer Sir George Mackenzie visited London in 1679, he did not hesitate to offer advice on composition to John Dryden, then England's Poet Laureate (and was politely thanked as 'that noble wit of Scotland'). Mackenzie took it for granted that they both inhabited the same culture-bubble. The novels of the Dumbartonshire-born Tobias Smollett, in the 18th century, are written within a British context, which assumes all his readers share basic tastes and the same cultural background. Publication of James Macpherson's 'Ossian' prose-poems in the 1760s opened a new, though as it happened phoney, dimension on the Scottish past, and the popularity of Robert Burns (after his death) and Sir Walter Scott did even more to change things. Though Burns could adopt a 'British' tone (*Does Haughty Gaul Invasion Threat?*) his work clearly stood within a Scottish tradition. Scott also revealed a country that was very evidently a different one from England, formed of its own experiences and with its own institutions. Paradoxically, Scott was a Unionist, as keenly aware of the kinships and resemblances as he was of the differences. Since Scott, novelists, playwrights and poets show a tacit

acknowledgement of a different playing field where the game was played using maybe not quite the same rules.

There are no great portrayals of English individuals in Scottish literature, and only three great portrayals of Scots in 'English' English literature: Macbeth and his wife, and Thomas Hardy's Donald Farfrae in *The Mayor of Caster-bridge*. Shakespeare's Scottish play was a compliment and sweetener to England's new king – by dint of some nifty genealogical tweaking,

Thomas Hardy

the ultimately victorious (with Northumbrian help) Malcolm was James VI and I's ancestor. Farfrae (how many English readers would click on the semi-joke 'far frae hame'?) wins friends on his first night in Casterbridge by singing nostalgic Scots songs, though one old fellow asks, 'What did ye come away from yer own country for, young maister, if ye be so wownded about it?' Donald does not reply directly, but has already said, 'I am on my way to ... the other side of the warrld, to try my fortune in the great wheat-growing districts of the West'. It is an interesting choice on Hardy's part: in 1830s Wessex a stranger from any other part of England would be considered a 'furriner', but a Scot even more so. But the novelist never forgets he is dealing with a Scot. Farfrae is the only person who faces up to the masterful and domineering Michael Henchard, and his openness and generosity of spirit contrast with Henchard's self-protective and ultimately fatal egoism. Hardy is not trying to make a point about Scots people in general: what is of interest is that he should create a Scot to match his brooding, powerful but fatally flawed Englishman. He was writing at a time when British imperialism was at its height and it's highly unlikely he was making any gesture towards Scotland: to pick a Scot merely added geographical emphasis to the differences between his two characters. A Scottish reader would want to know which part of the country Farfrae hails from, for Hardy it is enough that he is Scottish.

Scottish writing has no-one comparable to Farfrae. Sir Walter Scott, of course (long before Hardy) has a whole sequence of English heroes, from Edward Waverley to Ivanhoe and Francis Osbaldistone. Scott had a shrewd awareness of the size of the English reading market and its interest in its own native themes. But critics are united in observing that the psychological penetration deployed on his Scottish characters is much deeper than on his English ones. Robert

J.M.Barrie

Louis Stevenson contained an intense Scottishness within a cosmopolitan sensibility. J.M.Barrie revisited his origins in a more sentimental and nostalgic way, and – unlike Stevenson – his best work is English in all respects. There is nothing overtly Scottish in *Treasure Island*, any more than there is in *Peter Pan*; both came from Scottish minds that could adopt English tones with the effortless mimicry of a chameleon. Conan Doyle's Sherlock Holmes might be taken as a portrayal of a brilliant and eccentric Englishman, but he is modelled on an Edinburgh University professor. It is hard to think of an English equivalent that has the same degree of success – but it should not be forgotten that two cherished Scottish cartoon series, *The Broons* and *Oor Wullie*, were the creations of an Englishman, Dudley D. Watkins. The Scottish writer Allan Massie claims that: 'There is an over-arching British culture which has been created by the interaction of the different national cultures within the United Kingdom … To deny the reality of a British culture is folly, refusal to look reality in the face', but he could equally well have drawn in the contribution of the United States, which would have spoiled his diversity-within-union theme. Sometimes a Scottish work achieves recognition on its own terms within the British context, as when James Kelman won the Booker Prize in 1994 with *How Late it Was, How Late* (it was seen as a controversial choice). Scottish writers seem more fraught about this than musicians, actors or artists – in late 2011 battle was joined between those who see Scottish writing as too narrow and parochial in its interests and sensibilities, and those

who want to work through Scottish themes that are still live
and significant.

Two Footnotes on Culture

Englishman: Do you know why they are training Russian
cosmonauts in Scotland?
    Scotsman: No, why?
    Englishman: Because it has absolutely no atmosphere.

Scot, proudly: I suppose you know that it was a Scot who
developed penicillin?
    Englishman: Yes, it's the only culture a Scotsman ever
developed.

John Bull and Sister Peg

John Bull, the English archetype, was the creation of a Scot. Dr John Arbuthnot (1667–1735) was a witty medical man who had a taste for politics and for the literary life. He hailed originally from Arbuthnott, Kincardineshire, where his father had been the Episcopalian parson. A long-time resident of London, it was in 1712 that he created the persona of 'John Bull' to represent the typical Englishman, in *The Famous History of John Bull*, part of a series of satires written against the Duke of Marlborough. Arbuthnot drew a comparison between John Bull and his sister, 'poor Peg' (Peg being short for Margaret, at that time the most usual female name in Scotland):

> John Bull in the main was an honest plain-dealing fellow, choleric, bold, and of a very inconstant temper. He dreaded not old Lewis [France] … but then he was very apt to quarrel with his best friends, especially if they pretended to govern him. If you flattered him, you might lead him as a child.

John Bull, otherwise a good-natured man, was very hard-hearted to his sister Peg, chiefly from an aversion he had conceived in his infancy. While he flourished, kept a warm house, and drove a plentiful trade, poor Peg was forced to go hawking and peddling about the streets, and when she could not get bread for her family, she was forced to hire them out at journey-work to her neighbours. Yet in these poor circumstances she still preserved the air and mien of a gentlewoman, a certain decent pride, that extorted respect from the haughtiest of her neighbours; when she came in to any assembly, she would not yield the pass to the best of them. If one asked her, 'Are you related to John Bull?' 'Yes,' says she, 'he has the honour to be my brother.'

Arbuthnot's view was a kindly one, as befitted one of the first 'Anglo-Scots', Queen Anne's favourite doctor, according to Jonathan Swift, and a user of Augustan English prose who probably never wrote a word of Scots in his life. John Bull became a byword, but 'Sister Peg' did not catch on for Scotland. Scotland already had a female persona in Caledonia (not yet stern and wild). Anglia never took human shape: clearly any sort of feminine identity for the land of roast beef lacked conviction. Britannia, though familiar as a buxom lady sitting by a union-jack cheese – and, in *Rule Britannia*, saluted by a Scotsman, James Thomson – has remained a glacial, imperial figure devoid of personality.

Strangely enough, neither the Scots nor the English have a special derogatory term that applies to the other nation. With their strong sense of culinary conservatism, the English called the French 'Frogs' on account of their supposed eating habits. Germans, Italians, Spaniards and others were also favoured with special terms. The French retaliated at one time by calling the English 'les goddams', after the English soldiery's favourite epithet. But between Scotland and England, the blood was often bad enough for the mere word 'Scot' to be a term of abuse. By the eighteenth century, 'Scotch' was taking on a tinge of offensiveness south of the border, which is why it has largely dropped out of use, except when applied to whisky, broth and buttery sweets; and in the laborious jocularity of occasional English writers.

John Buchan
in search of spies

The Scottish word 'Sassenach', nowadays cheerfully used in a jokingly self-apologetic way by the English, has lost its sting in use for the Scots. Its original Gaelic form simply means 'Saxon', and was used in the Highlands to describe, not the English, but Scottish Lowlanders. But as most comments on the Saxon were in a context of complaint, insult or mockery, it acquired the same sort of taint as 'Scotch' did. 'Southron', the word used for English in Blind Harry's *Wallace*, also clearly had the same derogatory sense.

But just 'English' can be enough. In John Buchan's romance *Huntingtower*, the Scottish hero, Dickson McCunn, feels obliged to explain to an old lady the curious behaviour of his English ally, John Heritage: 'English', he says, significantly. No more needs to be said.

> I am glad to see you make a point of calling them 'Scotchmen' not 'Scotsmen' as they like to be called. I find this a good easy way of annoying them.
> George Orwell, letter to Anthony Powell (1936)

Old Wars, and Battles Long Ago

Invasion and warfare are invariably accompanied by a propaganda campaign, and usually followed up by rancour and anger on the part of the losers. The oldest traceable records of such exchanges between Scotland and England go back to the time of Edward I and Robert Bruce. An anonymous poet writing in Latin made the boast: *Unus Anglus perimet Scoticos quam plures* – 'One Englishman is worth many Scots', and another compared the Scots' struggle against Edward I to that of a pig rebelling against a lion:

> *Quasi sus insurgeret leonis virtuti,*
> *Sic expugnant Angliam Scotici polluti*

> 'As a pig might rise up against the splendour of the lion,
> so the dirty Scots fight against England.'

The patriotic English poet Laurence Minot has left a number of poems attacking the Scots, some of which hark back to events before his birth in 1333. In this he warns the traitorous Scots and their French allies not to mess with Edward Longshanks:

> The traytours of Scotlond token hem to rede [take counsel]
> The barouns of engeland to brynge to dede; [to do to death]
> Charles of fraunce, so mani men tolde,

with myht & with streynthe hem helpe wolde
                                        [would help them]
his thonkes!   [thanks to him!]
Tprot, Scot, for this strif!   [strife]
Hang up thyn hachet and thi knyfe,
Whil him lasteth the lyf,   [while he with the long shanks lives]
With the longe shonkes.

Following the Scottish victory at Bannockburn in 1314, an anonymous Scots bard jeered:

Maydens of Englande, sore may ye morne
For your lemmans ye have lost at Bannockysborne, [lovers]
With heve a lowe.
What, weneth the kynge of Englande   [thinks]
So soone to have wonne Scotlande?

After the English victory over the invading Scots at Halidon Hill in 1333, an equally anonymous versifier was able to hit back:

Scots out of Berwick and out of Aberdeen,
At the burn of Bannock ye were far too keen.
Many guiltless men ye slew, as was clearly seen,
But King Edward has avenged it now, and fully too, I ween.

... 'Tis now, thou rough-foot, brogue-clad Scot,
    that begins thy care,
Thou boastful barley-bag-man, thy dwelling is all bare.
False wretch and forsworn, whither wilt thou fare?

Blind Harry, the fifteenth-century poet who composed *The Wallace*, was bitterly anti-English – not surprisingly, considering the fate meted out to the hero of his poem. The poem was written at a time of renewed hostility with England: the enmity was not expressed with any degree of wit, but Harry was the original coiner of a phrase that has stuck in Scottish usage ever since:

> Our auld enemys of Saxony's blud
> That unto Scotland never sall do gud.

Scots played a substantial part, on the French side, in the campaigns and battles of the Hundred Years' War that gradually forced England out of its French possessions. At Baugé in 1421 a battle almost wholly between English and Scots was fought. It was not a major engagement but was well-remembered as a Scottish victory; the historian George Buchanan noted that the English 'took it in great disdain that they should be attacked by such an implacable enemy, not only at home but beyond the seas'. Henry V's death on campaign occurred after he had ordered the desecration of a shrine dedicated to St Fiacre, legendary son of a Scottish king (Gaelic Fiachra). Many believed the saint's curse struck him with leprosy – and he is said to have died cursing the Scots and saying 'I can go nowhere without finding Scotsmen, dead or alive, at my beard.'

Before the battle of Flodden in 1513, an anonymous Gaelic poet wrote verses of encouragement to the Earl of Argyll and his men:

> Against Saxons, I say to you,
> Lest they rule our country too,
> Fight roughly: like the Irish Gael
> We will have no English pale.

The English point of view was expressed in *Against the Scots*,

a diatribe by John Skelton, who flourished in the late fifteenth
and early sixteenth centuries. Written after the Scottish defeat
at Flodden, it mocks at the pride of the Scots, who appear to
have shown unwillingness to admit that they were beaten:

> Against the proud Scots clattering,
> That never will leave their tratling: [prattling]
> Won they the field, and lost their king?
> They may well say, fie on that winning!
> Lo, these fond sots
> And tratling Scots,
> How they are blind
> In their own mind,
> And will not know   [acknowledge]
> Their overthrow
> At Branxton Moor!
> They are so stour,
> So frantic mad,
> They say they had
> And won the field
> With spear and shield.
> That is as true
> As black is blue
> And green is grey.
> Whatever they say
> Jemmy is dead   [James IV]
> And closed in lead,
> That was their own king:
> Fie on that winning!

Skelton was able to have another go in 1532, when the Duke
of Albany made an ineffectual invasion of England with a
force of Scottish and French troops. His poem is sarcastically
entitled: 'How the Doughty Duke of Albany, like a coward

knight, ran away shamefully with an hundred tratling Scots and faint-hearted Frenchmen, beside the Water of Tweed'.

> This duke so fell
> Of Albany,
> So cowardly,
> With all his host
> Of the Scottish coast,
> For all their boast,
> Fled like a beast;
> Wherefore to jest
> Is my delight
> Of this coward knight ...
> Etc., etc.

Both Scots and English used to accuse each other of treachery, often for good reason. In times long past, neither side was

above breaking its word when it saw an advantage to be gained. In his *History of Greater Britain*, the sixteenth-century Scot John Mair notes: 'I have read in histories written by Englishmen that the Scots are the worst of traitors, and that this stain is inborn with them. Not otherwise, if we are to believe these writers, did the Scots overthrow the kingdom and the warlike nation of the Picts. The Scots, on the other hand, call the English the chief of traitors, and, denying that their weapon is a brave man's sword, affirm that all their victories are won by guile and craft.'

In February 1545, Henry VIII granted a vast extent of the Scottish borderland to Sir Ralph Evers, warden on the English side – if he could conquer it. The Scottish lieutenant of the borders was the Earl of Angus, who remarked: 'If they come to take sasine [right of possession] in my lands, I will write the deeds on their backs with sharp pens and bloody ink.' At the battle of Ancrum Moor, Evers' army was scattered by the Scots. Henry VIII made fulminations against Angus, who was unrepentant: 'Little knows King Henry the skirts of Cairntable. I can keep myself there against all his English host.' (But it was not there but at Pinkie on 'Black Saturday' in September 1547 that his army was routed by the Earl of Somerset's).

At the height of the Spanish Armada crisis in 1588, an advisor of the English state secretary, Walsingham, wrote to warn him that 'England will find Scotland, old Scotland still, and traitorous in the greatest need'.

During the 'Bishops' War' of 1638–40, the English poet Sir William Davenant wrote:

> We feared not the Scots from the High-land nor Low-land;
> Though some of their leaders did craftily brave us,
> With boasting long service in Russe and Poland,
> And with their fierce breeding under Gustavus.

Not the Tales of their Combats, more strange
    than Romances,
Nor Sandy's screw'd Cannon did strike us with wonder;
Nor their Kettle-drums sounding before
    their long Launces,
But Scottish-Court-Whispers struck surer than
    Thunder.

– it was the court intrigues of Scottish nobles that were really
to be feared. A whiff of treachery is in the air: the words 'rebel
Scot' always came readily to an English patriotic pen:

If ever England had occasion
Her ancient honour to defend,
Then let her now make preparation,
Unto an honourable end:
The factious Scot
Is very hot,
His ancient spleene is ne'er forgot
He long hath bin about this plot.

Our graytious Soveraigne very mildely
Did grant them what they did desire,
Yet they ingratefully and wildly
Have still continued the fire
Of discontent
'Gainst government,
But England now is fully bent,
Proud Jocky's bosting to prevent.
                – so ran part of *A True Subject's Wish*,
           from an anonymous supporter of King Charles I

English chauvinist prejudices were rampant. An English
officer in 1639 devoted several lines to a litany of hostile adjec-

tives that describe 'the scurvy, filthy, dirty, nasty, lousy, itchy, scabby, shitten, stinking, slovenly, snotty-nosed, villainous, barbarous, bestial, false, lying, roguish, devilish' Scots (Mark Stoyle, *Soldiers and Strangers*, 2006). But he and his colleagues had just been outfaced by the Scottish army in the first Bishops' War.

Just about the only time that the Scots created real fear in the English nation – apart from the short panic of late 1745 – was in the first half of the 1640s, when the Scottish army, invading England, was the strongest military force in the country until the New Model Army was formed. At first the Scots were allies of the English Parliament, but misunderstandings soon clouded matters, and a war of pamphlets carried accusations and counter-accusations backwards and forwards. A typical title was the Englishman John Lilburne's 'An Unhappy Game at Scotch and English, Wherein their Scotch Mists and their Fogs; their sayings and gainsaying; their Juglings, their windings and turnings hither and thither, backwards and forwards, and forwards, backward again … detected, discovered and presented to the View of the World as a dreadful Omen and Warning to the Kingdom of England'. Lilburne protested, in the kind of language more often used by Scots to the English, that 'we will maintain our just Rights and Freedomes in despite of Scots King, or Keysar, though wee welter for it in our blood; and bee it knowne unto you, o yee Men of Scotland, that the free-men of England scorne to bee your Slaves, and they have yet a reserve of gallant blood in their veines, which they will freely spend for their Freedom'.

Since 1746, Scottish and English soldiers have fought within the British Army, against other enemies than one another. Despite this, later Scottish ballads returned to the theme of Scottish–English warfare, as in Scott's 'All the Blue Bonnets are Bound for the Border':

Stand to your arms then and march in good order;
England shall many a day
Tell of the bloody fray
When the Blue Bonnets came over the Border.

Or again, in 'Wi' a Hundred Pipers':

Dumbfounder'd the English saw, they saw,
Dumbfounder'd the English ran awa' …

English poets did not share in this return to old history. Their martial bards (oddly enough, often Scotsmen) were more likely to sing of England's deeds on land and sea against the French.

The old British army system put Scots in Scottish regiments and English in English regiments. But increasingly there were units not linked to any country or region, like the Royal Army Ordnance Corps. In the Second World War, the nationalist-minded author George Campbell Hay wrote to Douglas Young of his experiences in the RAOC:

The Caledonians and South Britons mix no better than oil and water. If you ask about anyone and what sort of person he is the first classification is always 'He's wan o' they bloody Englishmen' or 'He's a Scotch bastard' and that's the natural attitude you get … The most notable characteristic about the English is how docile they are … But most of my compatriots, God be thankit, haven't the faintest trace of the spirit of subordination … One Aberdonian (we have plenty) eyed a nagging sort of sergeant significantly and said 'Did anyone ever hit ye afore, sergeant?'

Church and Kirk

One of the more bizarre aspects of the British Union is the ability of the monarch to be at the head of two quite distinct Churches, each set up as the 'established' form of Christianity in its own territory. In the seventeenth century, when such things were taken more seriously, the Scots started a war when King Charles I tried to change the constitution of their presbyterian Church. The English in turn forcibly resisted Scottish efforts to make them adopt the same system:

> The Scots themselves, that discontented Brood
> Who always loudest for Religion bawl,
> (As those still do wh'have none at all),
> Who claim so many Titles to be Jews,
> (But, surely, such whom God would never for
> his People chuse).

Jonathan Swift (1667–1745),
Ode to the King

At the time of the Union in 1707, the Archbishop of Canterbury remarked that although he believed the Church of Scotland was as true a Protestant Church as the Church of England, 'he could not say it was so perfect'. Sydney Smith claimed that he had studied the subject of the 'Scotch Church' in vain: 'I have not the smallest conception what it is about. I know it has something to do with oatmeal, but beyond that I am in utter darkness.' A Scottish ecclesiastic might have replied that utter darkness was the appropriate place for an Anglican, but Scottish churchmen of the time were not known for wit. Edmund Burt noted that a minister in Inverness, in the course of his sermon, urged his congregation to 'fly from the example of a wicked neighbouring nation' – the name was unspecified, but nobody thought he meant Ireland.

For those who compared the religious practice of both countries, the definite quality of Scottish thinking and the more diffuse form of English thought were often seized on: 'It is possible to attend all the places of worship of all the denominations from Berwick to the Lizard without gathering any very clear idea as to Who or What the Englishman thinks he is worshipping', wrote James Bridie, in *A Small Stir* (1949). Nobody skewered Scottish religious hypocrisy better than Robert Burns in *Holy Willie's Prayer*, but plenty others have had a go:

> A little Scottish building firm had gained a big contract, but there was a penalty clause on lateness. Work was falling behind and in order to get back on schedule, the owner paid his men extra to work on Sunday. As the workers got busy, he suddenly had a twinge of conscience:
>   'Don't hammer,' he called to them. 'Use screws.'

Divided by a Single Language

England has many dialects and regional accents, and the form of English that the Scots knew best for long was the Geordie tongue of Northumberland which shares many characteristics with Scots. But only two English accents are really acknowledged, the 'lah-di-dah' drawl of the upper classes, associated with the public school system and Oxford; and the h-less speech of the Cockney. Posh English is not so common now as it was when Moray McLaren, in 1949, said that someone talking this way 'really sometimes sounds like a music-hall turn'. He observed that 'Neither in Scotland nor in Ireland do we have this esoteric form of speech. So our people are not accustomed to other people speaking in a special sort of way because they write and think (sic) in a special way.'

The Scots have rarely been in doubt as to the quality of their own diction. Speaking of pleading at the bar, Sir George Mackenzie (1636–91) wrote: 'To me it appears undeniable that the Scotish idiom of the British tongue is more fit for Pleading than either the English idiom or the French tongue; for certainly a Pleader must use a brisk, smart and quick way of speaking; whereas the English, who are a grave nation, use a too slow and grave pronunciation ... Our Pronunciation is like ourselves, fiery, abrupt, sprightly and bold ... our Accent is natural, and has nothing, or at least little in it that is peculiar. I say this not to asperse the English, they are a Nation I honour, but to reprove the petulancy and malice of some amongst them, who think they do their Country good service, when they reproach ours.'

Let bragart England in disdain
Ha'd ilka lingo, but her ain:
Her ain, we wat, say what she can,
Is like her true-born Englishman,
A vile promiscuous mungrel seed
O' Danish, Dutch an' Norman breed,
An' prostituted since, to a'
The jargons on this earthly ba'!

Alexander Geddes (1737–1802),
Epistle to the Society of Antiquaries

At his first meal in Edinburgh, the early eighteenth-century traveller Edmund Burt claimed that the cook offered him the choice of: 'a duke, a fool, or a mere-fool. This was nearly according to his pronunciation; but he meant a duck, a fowl, or a moor-fowl, or grouse.'

Henry Mackenzie remembered an anecdote about Lord
Elibank, an early example of the Anglo-Scot, 'a great Scotsman
when in England, and a great Englishman when in Scotland'.
A neighbour of his in East Lothian was holding forth on the
superior qualities of the Scots.

'I don't dispute that,' said Elibank, 'but I think they [the
English] do one thing better.'

'You mean, my lord, they make better cheese, but I deny
that.'

'No, laird, I only think they speak better English.'

The eminent Scottish lawyer John Clerk of Eldin had to go
to London to plead before the House of Lords in a property
dispute. Clerk spoke with a Scottish accent and at one point
he used the word 'enow', the Scots form of 'enough'. The lord
chancellor, Lord Eldon, stopped him, saying, 'In England, Mr
Clerk, we sound the -ough as -uff – enough, not enow.'

'Verra weel, my Lord,' said Clerk. 'We have said enough
of that. I come now to the subdivision of the land in dispute.
It was apportioned, my Lord, into what in England you will
call pluff-land, a pluff-land being as much land as a pluff-man
will pluff in one day.' The lord chancellor interrupted him
again, with a laugh this time: 'I think I know enow of Scots
to follow your argument, Mr Clerk. Pray carry on.' No more
corrections were made.

A contributor to *Blackwood's Magazine* in 1817 recorded a
discussion in an Edinburgh bookshop, when he and a friend,
an author, were looking at an old Scots ballad.

'Let me entreat you, for God's sake, to make the language
of this ballad so as that we can understand it,' he said to his
friend.

'I carena whether ye understand it or no, min; I dinna aye
understand it very weel mysel.'

'It is not for what you or I, or any Scotsman, may understand; but remember this must be a sealed book to the
English.'

'O, it's a' the better for that – thae English folk like aye best
what they dinna understand.'

A nineteenth-century *Punch* cartoon showed a Cockney
tourist in a Scottish inn.

Cockney Tourist: I'll 'ave a bottle of ale.

Scottish Waitress: Will that be castor ile or paraffin ile, sir?

In the 1950s there were many complaints about the ultra-
English accents of BBC radio announcers in Scotland. The
poet and folklorist Hamish Henderson wrote in a letter to *The
Scotsman*: 'If an announcer pronounces "Boer War" with the
accent of Barra or the accent of Buchan, fair enough, but if
he pronounces "Boer War" as if he were a Pekingese barking
defiance (Baw waw! Baw waw!) he should be out on his neck.'
But language has many pitfalls:

On a draughty London Transport escalator, a pretty girl
was having trouble preventing her skirt from blowing
up.

'A bit airy, isn't it?' said a sympathetic visitor from
Scotland, a few steps below.

'What did you expect?' snapped the girl. 'Feathers?'

Scotland of course has also preserved another language
altogether, even if very few can speak it. In the eighteenth
century the assumption that they all spoke Gaelic was a little
more reasonable. When Mrs Margaret Stewart Calderwood
of Polton made a visit to England in 1756, at the inn at Barnet,
north of London, she was met by 'a squinting, smart-like black
girl', who spoke to her in what she took to be Irish:

'Are you a Highlander?'

'No,' said she, 'I am Welsh, are you not Welsh?'

'No,' said I, 'but I am Scots, and the Scots and the Welsh are near relations, and much better born than the English.'

'Oh!' said she, 'the maid said you was Welsh, and sent me to see you.'

She took me by the hand, and looked so kindly that I suppose she thought me her relation, because I was not English; which makes me think the English are a people one may perhaps esteem or admire, but they do not draw the affection of strangers, neither in their own country nor out of it.

A Stushie Between Historians

It is not only in sport that latter-day rivalries and spats occasionally break out between Scotland and England. A notable joust took place in the 1970s when the Scottish historian William Ferguson assailed the English historian Hugh Trevor-Roper (later Lord Dacre), following the publication of an essay on 'Scotland and the Puritan Revolution'. With phrases like 'Perhaps some-time they [Trevor-Roper and his followers] should descend from their airy theoretical heights to dart a glance at the evidence', Trevor-Roper's thoughts on the Scottish Reformation are dismissed by Ferguson as 'a mishmash of elementary points, none too accurately handled, strung together with rhetorical questions and garnished with burlesque humour. In his excursions into "Scotch history" he is very unkind to himself ... With his information so limited and his method of argument so defective, it is to be feared that Trevor-Roper's celebrated essay ... contains more to admire at than to admire.'

Trevor - Roper
takes on
Scottish history

A reader of this essay can certainly detect a patronising tone. When Trevor-Roper claims English historians' view of seventeenth-century Scotland to be 'a barbarous country populated only by doltish peasants manipulated, for their own factious ends, by ambitious noblemen and fanatical ministers', it is evident that he shares it. What really got up Trevor-Roper's nose seems to have been the patronising approach of the 'fanatical ministers' from Scotland. That such persons should come to England and presume to interfere with its ordering of religious practice offended him deeply, and he writes waspishly of such characters as Robert Baillie (admittedly a religious bigot of insufferable complacency), as if he were still around rather than dead for 300 years; and compares the reactions to London of one Presbyterian, Alexander Brodie, to those of a Bedouin transported to the splendours of Baghdad. Another Scottish historian, David Stevenson, gave a more formal demolition to Trevor-Roper's interpretation. Dacre died in 2003, but from beyond the grave, he returned to a Scottish theme with *The Invention of Scotland* (2008), an edited version of a project laid aside in 1982, presenting through 'the interaction of myth and history in Scotland' the thesis that it is 'Celtic Britain' which has provided all the national mythology of the British nations: 'The Anglo-Saxons … have been the least mythopoeic of peoples. The English have created one of the great literatures of the world. Yet, have they a single myth that they can call their own?' The notion is interesting, and the tone of the book less superior than before. But the thesis is a dubious one. Beowulf was certainly no 'Celt'.

The Intolerable Sense of Superiority of the English

The tone adopted by Professor Trevor-Roper in his ruminations on Scotland was not a new one. It was in the sixteenth century that English complacency really began to be expressed. William Harrison, in his *Description of England* (1577), wrote that the English are 'blessed in every waie, and there is temporall commoditie necessarie to be had or craved by any nation at God's hand that he hath not in most abundant manner bestowed on us Englishmen'.

In the next century, John Milton wrote: 'It is in God's manner to reveal Himself first to his Englishmen.' From such

a thought it was but a short step to the 'God is an Englishman' view. As the English writer Paul Langford notes, of other peoples' view of the English: 'They assumed that what drove them was a unique, or at any rate insular, sense of destiny based more on arrogance than moral superiority. The essence of the claim was not so much that the English reasoned that they were superior to others but that it genuinely did not occur to them that any rational being could suppose they were anything else ... To be born an Englishman implied an act of divine grace that left its beneficiaries profoundly grateful.'

Remember that you are an English-man and have consequently won first prize in the lottery of life.

Cecil Rhodes (1853–1902)

Cecil Rhodes

The English have never bothered to define their national identity. Instead there are phrases: the tautologous 'we know who we are,' or the comfortable 'we govern ourselves pretty decently.'

Neal Ascherson,
Games with Shadows (1988)

The Intolerable Sense of Superiority of the Scots

'Here's tae us! Wha's like us? Damn few, and they're a' deid.' The wha's like us? attitude of the Scots has irritated not only the English; the old French phrase *fier comme un Ecossais* was not necessarily a compliment. Scotch superiority could be delivered with over-oiled unction: 'Minds like ours, my dear James, must always be above national prejudices, and in all companies it gives me true pleasure to declare that, as a people, the English are very little indeed inferior to the Scotch',

proclaimed 'Christopher North' (John Wilson, 1785–1854), in *Blackwood's Magazine*.

Tongue well in cheek, James Bridie wrote: 'The Scots have always been famed for their dignified humility. They know themselves to be perfervidly ingenious and to be the admiration and envy of all other peoples. It would be most shocking if they were addicted to rubbing it in. They can be tolerant of and even amused at the Englishman's pretensions to having a Scottish great-grandmother'.

'I was born a true Englishman, all my life I've been a true Englishman, and I hope to die a true Englishman,' proclaimed the – needless to say – Englishman.

'Man, have ye nae ambeetion?' inquired his Scottish friend.

Mr Boswell's Bear

Perhaps the most famous and articulate of all Scottophobes was Dr Samuel Johnson (1709–84). But Johnson's anti-Scots pronouncements have only been preserved through the obsessive attention of his Scottish friend and biographer, James Boswell, who insisted that the great Englishman was not anti-Scottish at all. Boswell (1740–85) was convinced that Johnson's famous animosity to the Scots was caused by his reaction to the Scots' own nationalistic fervour. He quotes Johnson as saying to an acquaintance: 'When I find a Scotchman, to whom an Englishman is as a Scotchman, that Scotchman shall be as an Englishman to me.' Yet he was also obliged to admit that Johnson 'considered the Scotch, nationally, as a crafty, designing people, eagerly attentive to their own interest, and too apt to overlook the claims and pretentions of other people'.

More than most London Scots of the eighteenth century, Boswell suffered from a confused sense of national identity. His instincts and most of his attitudes were Scottish: his inclinations were English. He was one of those who tried vainly to establish the common term 'Briton', with its 'North' and 'South' division. A faithful if sometimes inadvertent chronicler of his own failings, Boswell has never been quite forgiven by his compatriots for his self-revelation in his very first conversation with Johnson:

Boswell: I do indeed come from Scotland, but I cannot
    help it.
Johnson: That, Sir, I find, is what a very great many of
    your countrymen cannot help.

This first exchange set the tone for many subsequent John-
sonian gibes:

'The noblest prospect which a Scotchman ever sees is
the high road that leads him to England.'

'We have taught you (said he) and we'll do the same in
time towards all barbarous nations, – to the Cherokee
–, and at last to the Orang-Outangs.'

'Much may be made of a Scotchman, if he be caught
young.'

'Your country consists of two things, stone and water.
There is, indeed, a little earth above the stone in some
places, but a very little, and the stone is always
appearing. It is like a man in rags; the naked skin is still
peeping out.'

Often Johnson was merely baiting his friend by his comments,
but his fundamental disapproval of the Scots does appear to
rest on what he called their 'extreme nationality': their clan-
nishness and mutual support – based not on personal merit
but merely on being fellow-Scots. Even on his celebrated visit
to Scotland, he did not hesitate to take issue with them, as in
his riposte to a critic of the Union with England:

James Kerr: Half our nation was bribed by English
    money.

Dr Johnson: Sir, that is no defence. It makes you worse.

Many Scots were determined not to be over-impressed by their distinguished visitor. The writer Henry Mackenzie noted that: 'When Boswell was bear-leading Johnson through Scotland, he introduced him, in the Parliament House at Edinburgh, to Henry Erskine, who, after making his bow and a short conversation left the conductor and conducted, putting a shilling into Boswell's hand, being the common fee for a sight of wild beasts.'

Some Reflections on the Union

Blest Revolution, which creates
Divided Hearts, united States.

Jonathan Swift (1667–1745)

Black be the day that e'er to England's ground
Scotland was eikit by the Union's bond.   [linked]

Robert Fergusson (1750–1774)

It is true, that we elect very near a twelfth part of the British House of Commons; but our representatives have no title to vote, or act in a separate body ... What therefore can 45 persons accomplish, when opposed by 513?

James Thomson Callendar,
The Political Progress of Britain, 1792

Scotland has long groaned under the chains of England and knows that its connection there has been the source of its greatest misfortunes ... We have existed a conquered province these two centuries. We trace our bondage from the Union of the Crown and find it little alleviated by the Union of the Kingdoms ... the Friends of Liberty in Scotland have almost universally been enemies to Union with England.

Lord Daer (1793)

Nothing can prevent the gradual disappearance of local manners under the absorption and assimilation of a far larger, richer and more powerful adjoining kingdom.

Henry Cockburn, *Journals*, 1853

The Scots are a very interesting mob in as much as they made a very interesting deal with the English. A sane deal. It had a lot of problems to it, but the alternative was to have these bastards come up here and kick your arse every twenty-five years.

Alan Sharp (1934–)

The relation the Scots have to the English is a symbiotic one and giving it up is psychologically very difficult because it's going to take away your excuse. With the English there we can say, 'if it wisnae for them bastards …'

Alan Sharp

Margaret Thatcher, who as prime minister did so much to contribute to the growth of Scottish nationalism, had this to say in February 1990, in the course of a debate on whether Scotland gained or lost economically by the Union: 'We English, who are a marvellous people, are really very generous to the Scots.'

Sir Bernard Ingham

Her press officer, Sir Bernard Ingham, put his own gloss on her thoughts, in April of the same year: 'The Scots are subsidised to the damned hilt. The first thing is to stop the Scots grumbling. Emasculate them. That would concentrate their minds. The Scots are getting too much.'

On reading this, one is somehow reminded of a remark by an Irishman, Cyril Connolly, who described the English as 'sheep with a nasty side'.

… the incapacity of an intensely self-centred English discourse to conceive of 'Britain' as anything but an enlargement of England.

J.C.A. Pocock, in Roger Mason (ed.),
Scots and Britons, 1994

Afterword

If it is possible to draw any conclusion from the centuries of co-habitation, confrontation and collaboration, it must be that the Scots and the English have some very different character-istics. At its simplest, the English attitude to life is that it is a game, which must be played in the correct spirit and according to a set of rules which is never published but everyone is supposed to understand. The referee is 'public opinion'. Because it's a game, there will always be winners. Life is not seen as a game by the Scots: rather it is a perpetual confrontation with forces beyond human control – Fate perhaps. In that encounter, humanity may be allowed occasional successes, enough to keep a positive spirit, but the ultimate winner is never in doubt. Together the two nations made a United Kingdom which rose on empire and industri-alism, both of which have receded beyond recall. A new future has to be constructed. Will these two peoples, so similar and so different, choose to make it together, or decide that their relationship must amicably change to allow each its own full expression in a very different world?

A Select Bibliography

Ascherson, Neal, *Games with Shadows*. London, 1988

Boswell, James, *The Life of Dr Samuel Johnson*. London, 1791

Bridie, James and McLaren, Moray, *A Small Stir: Letters on the English*. London, 1949

Bruce, George, and Scott, Paul H., *A Scottish Postbag*. Edinburgh, 1986

Burt, Edmund, *Letters from a Gentleman in the North of Scotland*. Edinburgh, 1998

Colley, Linda, *Britons*. London, 1992

Davies, C., *Ethnic Humour*. Bloomington, Ind., 1990

Ferguson, William, *Scotland's Relations with England*. Edinburgh, 1977

Fraser, George Macdonald, *The Steel Bonnets*. London, 1971

Gibbon, Lewis Grassic, and MacDiarmid, Hugh, *Scottish Scene*. London, 1934

Hume Brown, P., *Early Travellers in Scotland*. Edinburgh, 1891

Kamm, Anthony, and Leane, Anne, *A Scottish Childhood*. London, 1985

Kratzmann, G., *Anglo-Scottish Literary Relations, 1430–1550*. Cambridge, 1980

Langford, Paul, *Englishness Identified*. Oxford, 2000

Lindsay, Maurice, *The Discovery of Scotland*. London, 1964

MacDiarmid, Hugh, *Lucky Poet*. London, 1943

Massie, Allan, *The Thistle and the Rose*. London, 2004

Ross, David, *Scotland: History of a Nation*. Edinburgh, new
    ed 2010
Ross, David (ed.), *Scottish Quotations*. Edinburgh, 2000
Smith, W. Gordon, *This is My Country*. London, 1981
Trevor-Roper, Hugh, *The Invention of Scotland*. London,
    2011

Index of Personal Names

Arbuthnot, Dr John, 112, 113

Askwith, Betty 61,

Ascherson, Neal, 39, 43, 134, 145

Banks, Iain, 15

Barber, Peter, 61

Barrie, Sir J.M., 110

Benson, Theodora, 61

Blackie, John Stuart, 34, 62

Blind Harry, 69, 114, 116

Boorde, Andrew, 62

Borrow, George, 71

Boswell, James, 66, 67, 137–9

Brenan, Gerald, 41

Brereton, Sir William, 88

Bridie, James, 22, 39, 62, 66, 101, 125, 136

Buchan, John, 42, 114

Buchanan, George, 117

Buckle, Henry Thomas, 10, 11, 62

Bunting, Madeleine, 6

Burnet, Gilbert, 62

Burns, Robert, 4, 69, 108, 125

Burt, Edmund, 82, 88, 125, 127

Burton, John Hill, 99

Bute, Lord, 19, 30, 31, 98

Caesar, Julius, 8, 55

Calderwood, Margaret Stewart, 129

Cameron, David, 6, 14

Carlyle, Thomas, 63

Chapman, George, 28

Churchill, Charles, 31, 77, 98

Clerk, John, 128

Cleveland, John, 63

Colley, Linda, 98

Crosland, T.W.H., 76–7

Cryer, Barry, 45

Daer, Lord, 140

Dante, 16

Defoe, Daniel, 63

Derwent, Lavinia, 70

Douglas, Norman, 63, 88

Dunbar, William, 21